Curtis Guild

Britons and Muscovites

Traits of two empires

Curtis Guild

Britons and Muscovites
Traits of two empires

ISBN/EAN: 9783337174712

Printed in Europe, USA, Canada, Australia, Japan

Cover: Foto ©Andreas Hilbeck / pixelio.de

More available books at **www.hansebooks.com**

BRITONS AND MUSCOVITES

OR

TRAITS OF TWO EMPIRES

BY

CURTIS GUILD

EDITOR OF THE BOSTON COMMERCIAL BULLETIN, AUTHOR OF
"OVER THE OCEAN" AND "ABROAD AGAIN"

BOSTON
LEE AND SHEPARD PUBLISHERS
10 MILK STREET, NEXT OLD SOUTH MEETING-HOUSE
NEW YORK CHARLES T DILLINGHAM
1888

COPYRIGHT, 1888, BY CURTIS GUILD

All Rights Reserved

BRITONS AND MUSCOVITES

PREFACE.

IN presenting a third volume of experiences abroad, or the sights and scenes of foreign travel as seen by an American tourist, the author begins with that ever prolific field, England.

The reader is taken to the picturesque old ruins of Fountains and Furness Abbeys, to old Boston in Lincolnshire, and other historic points neglected by most travellers in that "tight little island." Some space is given to the consideration of English hotel management, from the fact that it seemed to be a leading topic with all American tourists. The abortive efforts to carry on large hotels in London on the American plan, and the annoyances experienced by Americans, who expect the same conveniences and accommodation obtainable at home, offer a tempting theme for general discussion.

A descriptive sketch is given of the author's journey to Russia, and the result of his observation of cities visited in that country, in the style which characterizes the description in his former volumes — of "Over the Ocean," and "Abroad Again."

This is done with a desire to be of service to those who may come after the author, to whom much of the minutiæ of description and many of the hints to tourists may be of service. In fact, the author, while seeking to avoid anything of the set guide-book character in his volume, has endeavored to render it of service to travellers, by presenting facts respecting the localities visited, such as cannot be found in any guide-book.

If in any degree he shall have succeeded in accomplishing this object, and, possibly, in entertaining with pen-pictures those unable to visit the scenes described, he will be more than gratified.

CONTENTS.

CHAPTER I.

Ubiquitous Americans — Methods of Travel — A Huge Steamship — Power and Dimensions — Life at Sea — Homage to Title — A Useful Institution — American Improvements — Liverpool and American Ideas 1

CHAPTER II.

A London Newspaper — Free Trade and Fair Trade — English Hotels — Cast-Iron Rules — Poor Clerks and Slow Servants — The Metropole and the Grand Hotels — Cold Reception — English Delay *vs.* American Impatience — How Not to Do It — Useless Officials — Clumsiness Personified — Cold Comfort and a Lean Larder 13

CHAPTER III.

The English Bill of Fare — American and British Menus Compared — Grand Hotel, London, and Fifth Avenue, New York — French Flummery — English Hotel Book-Keeping — A Most "Ex-twardinawy" Affair — Tyranny of Dress — Blunders of Travellers — Difference Between the English and American Language — American Drinks — Sherry Chickens — Astonishing a Publican — American Taverns and English Inns 25

CHAPTER IV.

Letter from an Englishman — The Author's Reply — An American Merchant's Views — Old-Fashioned Hotel Management — Lack of Modern Conveniences — Typical English Inn — Curious Mistake — English Shops — The Guinea Exaction — Fortunes of a Bibliopole 41

CHAPTER V.

A Trip to Ripon — Fountains Abbey — Charming Landscape Effects — Picturesque Ruins — Interesting Remains — Luxuries of a Monastery — The Great Hall — Ripon Cathedral — Superb Decorations — Robin Hood's Well — A Millennial Festival — An Antique Pageant — Old England Represented 53

CHAPTER VI.

Furness Abbey — A Romantic Glen — A Powerful Community — An Abbot-King — Remains of Architectural Beauty — Superb East Window — The Tower and Scriptorium — The Guest-Hall — Suppression of the Abbey — A Memorable Monastery — Glories of the Past 65

CHAPTER VII.

A Look into Lincolnshire — Old Boston — John Cotton and his Work — St. Botolph's Church — Its History — A Beautiful Tower — Fine Stone Carving — Chancel and Ancient Stalls — The East Window — Cotton Chapel — The American Tablet — Dimensions of St. Botolph's — An Old English Town — Shodfriars' Hall — Modern Improvements 73

CHAPTER VIII.

Boston to Berlin — The American Exchange — A Staid German City — Preparations for Trip to Russia — Railway Fares, Guide-Books, and Refreshments — The Smoking Nuisance — Travelling Companions — Arrival at the Frontier — Passports — Value of Deference to Officials — Baggage Examination — Railroad Restaurants — Experiences on the Line — Arrival at St. Petersburg — Fine Hotel — Press Censorship — Russian Illiteracy — Shop-Keeper's Curious Signs . 83

CHAPTER IX.

The Nevski Prospect — Fine Accommodations and Fair Prices — Novel Sights — Street Shrines and Worshippers — Costumes and Droskies — Grand Squares and Splendid Buildings — Churches and Palaces — The St. Nicholas Bridge — Quays, Bridges, and Canals — The Russian Army — St. Isaac's Cathedral — The Grand Entrances — An Architectural Wonder — Barbaric Splendor — Exquisite Stone-Work, Gold, Silver, Malachite, Lapis-lazuli, Marble, and Porphyry in Profusion — The Religious Ceremonies — Begging Nuns and Monks — Income of Monasteries — Sales of Religious Goods 95

CHAPTER X.

Petersburg the Paris of Russia — Beautiful Bridges — Cathedral of Our Lady of Kazan — Cossacks of the Guard — Meeting of the Grand-Duke Michael — An Immense Cathedral — Captured Trophies — A Rich Screen — The Wonderful Portrait — Seeing the Czar — Exchange Salutations at Ten Paces — An Unusual Piece of Good-Fortune — The Winter Palace — Peter the Great's Throne-Room — The Hermitage — A Wonderful Collection of Pictures — Fine Works of Great Artists — The Gallitzin Gallery — Priceless Archæological Treasures — The Grecian Helmet Holding the Owner's Head — Curious Antiques — Jewelry and Vases — Ancient Coins — A Feast for Artist, Archæologist, Antiquary, or Numismatist 109

CHAPTER XI.

Peter the Great — Reverence of him in Russia — Relics of him and his Time — Collection of Snuff-Boxes — Gems and Jewelry — Antiques and Rich Rarities of Every Kind — The Green Vaults Rivalled — A Model Guide — A Hint to Tourists — An Amusing Case — Escorted to the Frontier — Politeness of the Police to an American Offender — Museum of Imperial Carriages — Peter the Great's Sledge — Luxurious Chariot of Catherine II. — Alexander II.'s Carriage as Smashed by Nihilist Bombs — The Unfossilized Remains of Mastodons from Siberia — Ethnographic Exhibition — Peter the Great's Monument — Cathedral of St. Peter — Russian Saints — Catherine II. and her Monument — Peter the Great's Cottage — Peter's Summer Palace — Monastery of Alexander Nevski — Death-Bed of Peter — Altar-Screens — A Miniature Palace — Wonderful Wealth of Russian Churches — Peterhof Palace — The Imperial Summer Palace — The Royal Chapel — The Wonderful Amber Room — The Chinese Room — Room of Catherine II. — Prodigal Luxuriance — The Alexander Palace 121

CHAPTER XII.

From St. Petersburg to Moscow — A More Foreign Look — Moscow a Manufacturing City — Russian Cotton — Finances of the Country — Street Scenes in Moscow — Curious Vehicles — Monks and Nuns — Conflagration of Moscow — A City of Churches — The Kremlin — The Redeemer's Gate — The Big Bell — The Tower of Ivan — The Spoils of War — Napoleon's Cannon — The Arsenal — Great Riding-School — Cathedral of the Assumption — A Picture Decorated with a Quarter of a Million Dollars Worth of Jewels — Heaps of Precious Stones — Church of Archangel Michael — Tomb of Ivan the Terrible — The Treasury — Armor and Trophies — The Crowns and Thrones of Departed Monarchs — Another Prodigal Display of Wealth — Coronation Robes and Plate — The Carriage Museum — The Patriarch's Sacristy — The Sacred Oil and How it is Made — House of the Holy Synod — Illimitable Wealth in Precious Stones — Masterpieces of Art 144

CHAPTER XIII.

The Church in the Wood — St. Basil the Beautiful — Cathedral of St. Saviour — A New Memorial Temple — Grand Proportions, Rich Marbles, and Costly Carving — Visiting the Sanctum Sanctorum — How it was Accomplished — The Foundling Hospital — A Wonderful Institution — Training of the Inmates — Admirable System — Government Grant —

Illegitimacy in Russia — The Ride to Sparrow Hills — Fine
Panoramic View — Napoleon and Moscow — Recalling His-
toric Events on the Spot of their Enactment — Russian
Peasants — Siberian Exiles — Their March and Treatment . 166

CHAPTER XIV.

An Escape from Siberia — The Story of a Political Exile — The
Arrest — Farewell to Friends — The March — Guards, Food,
and Treatment — A Disguised Friend — Plans of Deliver-
ance — The Escape — Hardships and Risks in Reaching the
Frontier — Narrow Escape — America Reached at Last —
Another Exile — A Wood-Cutter in the Forests of Siberia —
He Turns Out to be a Learned College Professor — Meets
Two of his Former Pupils — The Sweets of Liberty . . . 181

CHAPTER XV.

Russian Post-Office Regulations — Simonof Monastery — A Once
Powerful Institution — All Asleep — The Great Bell-Tower
— Built for Defence — Wall and Watch-Towers — The
Romanoff House — Antique Russian Style — Curious Relics
— Work for Tourists — The Royal Palace — Standards of
the Russian Army — Grand Apartments — Halls of St.
George, St. Andrew, St. Alexander, and St. Catherine —
The Granite Palace — The Red Staircase — A Historic Spot
— Royal Banquet-Room — Mementos of Bonaparte's Inva-
sion — Traveller's Stories of Nijni Novgorod Fair — The
Railway Trip from Moscow to Nijni Novgorod 193

CHAPTER XVI.

Scenes at Nijni Novgorod — Miles of Wharves and Mountains of
Merchandise — Russian Beggars — Religious Pilgrims —
Fleets of Freight-Steamers — The Iron-Market — Russian
Iron — Wool and Cotton Marts — The Tea-Quarter — Tea
Testers and Tasters — Tartar Laborers — The Horse-Fair —
Orloff Horses — Turkish and Persian Fabrics — Vast Collec-
tion of Merchandise — The Turkish Quarter — Entering a
Turkish Mosque — An Obliging Mollah — Mussulman Beg-
gars — Precautions Against Fire 205

CHAPTER XVII.

The Cheap Quarter — Dust-Bin of the Empire — Raree-Shows and Cheap Exhibitions — Dance-Houses and Music-Halls — The Man-Eating Savages — A Cannibal Selling Photographs and Speaking English — A Surprised Showman — Tea-Drinking in Russia — Vodki-Shops — Business During the Fair — Russian Merchants Represented — The Daily Exchange — Russian Grain-Trade — A Clever Ruse — Russian Honesty — Drosky-Drivers — Shops — Travelling — Russia's Extent of Territory — Her Power and Possibilities 218

BRITONS AND MUSCOVITES;

OR

TRAITS OF TWO EMPIRES.

CHAPTER I.

THE Americans are said to be an uneasy race, from the fact that, go where you will, in any quarter of the globe, you are sure to meet them, and that more frequently than the natives of any other country.

It is a well known fact that London, Paris, Vienna, Switzerland, Rome, and other European localities depend on American visitors during the travelling season for increasing the business of their retail tradesmen, their hotels and travel routes. Indeed, a falling-off of American travel, owing to business panic or any other reason, is noted at once in European capitals and the consequent loss of trade commented on, both by tradesmen and the press. Again, the investigating spirit of the American, his thirst for something new, his desire to see something beyond what others have seen, to go farther, run greater risks, travel more miles or at greater speed than others have done before him, sends him to the uttermost parts of the earth and causes him to pervade the world generally.

American travellers are as plentiful all over Europe as flies at a sugar barrel. They wander through England's castles and abbeys, throw money away prodigally in Paris, applaud at bull fights in Spain, secure the best rooms in the Swiss hotels to the disgust of the plaid-suited and thick-shod Englishmen, scare their guides half out of their wits by their acts at the crater of Vesuvius, abuse custodians of the Vatican at Rome, ride like mad through the streets of St. Petersburg, charter unnecessary donkeys in Cairo, pay double price for curiosities at Thebes, get into difficulties in the crooked streets of Damascus, shoot alligators in Florida, dash in carioles over the mountain roads of Norway, meander through Mexico, steam along the gold-laden rocks of Alaska, and elbow their way round the streets of Melbourne.

In fact, Dr. Livingstone, the African explorer, who fancied that his was the only pale face among the ebony-hued natives of what he supposed was unknown Africa, must have been astonished, in that *terra incognita*, at seeing an individual advance with the American flag and the greeting: —

"Dr. Livingstone, I believe."

The Americans, by their continual pushing about, have done much to improve means of travel, to introduce conveniences, comforts, and facilities of their invention, often temporarily used by foreigners to please their visitors, but finally permanently adopted for themselves.

Notwithstanding it is now as much the fashion to examine and praise new American inventions as it used to be to decry and abuse them, yet there is something so clumsy and awkward in the English manner of trying to do anything after the American plan as to make Americans who suffer by it wish it had never been attempted. On the other hand, the pertinacity with which the English cling to customs obsolete elsewhere drives the bright, wide-awake Yankee, who is detained, hampered, and annoyed thereby, almost to the verge of desperation.

It is so much the fashion to travel nowadays, and there are so many methods by which what were formerly long, costly, and somewhat dangerous tours have been rendered enjoyable, cheap, and safe pleasure-trips, that almost all persons of moderate means can make or have made extensive tours at home or abroad. The Cook and Gaze tourist tickets, in Europe, and the better and perfectly managed Raymond excursions, here in the United States, remove a greater part of the burden and bother of travel, and really give to the tourist nearly all his time for the sight-seeing and enjoyment of his trip without the annoyances of ticket-buying, luggage-checking, and hotel arrangements, which necessarily fall to one's lot when travelling independently upon his own account.

Nevertheless, the latter method has its advantages to those who have the time and means to use it. The English are notorious grumblers as tourists, and prone to cavil at everything that does not exactly suit them; but if there is any one country in which the average American has reason to expect so much advance in the way of convenience and accommodation to the traveller, and finds so little, it is England.

Going over the ocean to-day in one of the great Cunard steamers is, however, very different and more speedy than it was twenty years ago. Then the author thought the voyage good and speedy in the old side-wheeler Asia, which accomplished the journey between Boston and Queenstown in twelve days! Now from the stepping on board the great steamer Umbria, at her pier in New York, to the stepping off at Liverpool, including the stop at Queenstown, the time was found to be exactly seven days and five hours — about half that covered by the first mentioned voyage.

A look at this huge specimen of naval architecture at the wharf, while exciting the wonder of the beholder, somehow or other gives him an impression prejudicial to her safety in a storm or heavy sea. You wonder if it may not be difficult or dangerous to manage such a huge affair, if something will not give out to render the leviathan an unmanageable mass at the mercy of the waves. A single voyage in rough weather, however, will change one's doubts into the belief, as it did mine, that this giant of navigation is a paragon of safety and comfort, as far as comfort can ever be said to be experienced by those who cross the ocean.

Owing to the size of the ship and the enormous power of her machinery, there is steadiness to her in comparatively rough seas that in smaller vessels would cause rolling and pitching to a marked degree. Then, the wide stairways, spacious, very spacious cabins, grand dining-hall, music-hall, ladies' private cabin, smoking and card room and servants' cabin, and withal the great promenade deck, broad, wide, and long — the length of the ship is very nearly one-tenth of a mile — make a fair-weather passage on one of these ocean greyhounds luxurious travelling indeed.

Ah! but how is it in rough and stormy weather?

Well, the ship, by reason of her immense power of machinery, does not remain long in the locality where the storm prevails; it is not with these ships as was the case with sailing vessels and slow steamers which made but a few miles a day and consequently remained long in the radius of a storm. This big ship, in a storm that sent waves away over her upper deck and the spray to the top of her enormous funnels, rolled and was unsteady, and the weather sent two-thirds of her passengers to their state-rooms sea-sick; but she kept right on, cut right through storm, wave, and tempest, on, on; — no tacking or stopping or finding that we were detained by the storm, but when the steward, with a cup of porridge, staggered to our state-room the next morning, it was with the cheerful intelligence that the run for the day just ended was 245 miles, and that ten hours more would carry us entirely clear of the storm-belt there prevailing. Best of all, his prediction was fulfilled.

Though we were all day below, the steady and rapid progress of the great ship, and the comparatively little effect which wind and wave had upon her as she faced, encountered, and overcame both with such ease, gave us a feeling of safety which we could not have so fully experienced in a ship of less power, and, we may perhaps add, less skilfully managed.

The dimensions of such ships as the Etruria and Umbria, of the Cunard line, fairly stagger those unacquainted with the size to which steamship-building has been carried in this nineteenth century. They are, in fact, the natural results of all that has been done in the development of ocean-going steaming, especially Atlantic steaming, for the past thirty years.

The gradual development of the lines of ocean-going steamers to the proportions of the yacht, combined with the adoption of well tested new methods, have reduced the designing of high speed to matters of certainty. This ship has made the trip to Queenstown in six days, fourteen hours, twenty minutes, and on another occasion in six days, eleven hours, and ten minutes, and it is expected to bridge the Atlantic in six days. The engines of this ship are a magnificent sight and in perfection of simplicity; they are said to be the most powerful in use.

The great breadth of the vessel has provided an abundance of room round their tremendous proportions, and the sight of the massive cranks revolving with perfect smoothness and regularity, at a speed of sixty-seven revolutions a minute, is interesting and wonderful. The horse-power of the engines here reached is something over one thousand two hundred and fifty, which is a trifle over the minimum, the maximum not having been reached at the time the author made his voyage.

The Umbria is 520 feet long, 57 feet broad, 41 feet deep, and of over eight thousand tonnage. She is the largest steamer afloat. The City of Rome is forty feet longer, but the Umbria is five feet broader and four feet deeper, and it is in depth and breadth that sea-sick people find comfort and consolation, and the steadiness of this ship is a most agreeable feature. The great breadth of the vessel gives room for the spacious staircases I have alluded to, which are as broad as those of a first-class hotel, and the means of access from one deck to the other are numerous as well as broad. The great saloon, extending from side to side, is 76 feet long and nine feet high, and is lighted from a cupola skylight above, which also lights a sitting or music room above, through the centre of which the light descends. At night the whole is lighted by incandescent electric lights, placed near the ceiling so that the view is not obstructed, thus replacing the odorous and even dangerous oil-lamp so loathed by qualmish passengers.

I do not recall the number of state-rooms in the

Umbria, but she can carry 720 first-class passengers, and on the trip we made in her there were 565 first-class passengers, yet the size of the ship was such that it was difficult to realize that there were half that number on board, except in smooth weather, at dinner-time, when they were brought together at the two dinners in the great cabin, one set dining at 5 and the other at 6 P. M. I mention details respecting the size and accommodations of this great vessel as illustrating what has thus far been accomplished to render the journey across the ocean comfortable as well as speedy.

The lines of the ship are unusually fine; she does not by any means look her size, and the disturbance of the water-way when at her greatest speed is comparatively trivial. The two funnels, upon which eighteen extra braces were put during one of our experiences of a two-days blow, are gigantic affairs, and three ordinary-sized men could stand one above the other within their diameter. The upper deck extends the whole breadth of the ship, obstructed only by the necessary hatchways and twelve life-boats, a space of 300 feet by 57 feet.

Everything is on a gigantic scale as compared with other steamers I have voyaged in; here was a huge air-pump that forced fresh air along the whole length of the corridors on the lower decks, through iron shafts perforated with holes an inch in diameter and two feet apart. By the force of this artificial current the ventilation is continuous and uniform in all weathers, and none of what is known as the between-deck odor is observable. The huge steam-boilers, the hull of the vessel, the crank-shaft and the more vital parts of the engine are all of steel. A feature of the great boilers that I had never seen before is that they were double-ended, that is, they had a set of furnaces at each end.

As steamers have increased in size and speed, the boiler has grown in size; but it has grown in circumference, not in length. The Umbria consumes three hundred tons of coal per day, and the total of her crew, including firemen, sailors, stewards, coal-passers, etc., is two hundred and eighty men. Although so much has been done in the past score of years as regards speed, convenience, and comfort, yet in the latter characteristic there is still much room for improvement in the matter of *cuisine* and attendance, and, I doubt not, it will be closely studied.

The majority of people making the voyage are seasick, at least for a portion of the time, and, though having the best of attention from stewards and stewardesses, could be still better served by a little departure from the old, established way of doing things, which has prevailed so many years on the ships of the Cunard line. For instance, the hours for meals were: breakfast, 8 o'clock; lunch, 1 to 2: dinner at 5. Thus the patient or the hungry convalescent must wait from 8 to 5 for a hot meal, for at lunch only cold meats are served. One wakes very early in the morning at sea, and it is a terrible time to wait until 8 o'clock for the warm breakfast. Again, the best of beef-tea, oatmeal-porridge, Oolong tea, and hot gruel ought to be kept on tap at all hours, and just as easily attainable by seasick passengers as liquors or wines.

A writer on ocean-voyages has written at length against passengers being obliged to furnish their own steamer-chairs, but this feature I think a good one as it enables one to provide for his own exclusive use such as he may desire. The price of this exclusive comfort is very small, and the opportunities, on a big ship like the Umbria, of removing one's couch or seat from point to point of observation, and always being sure of it, are many and afford entertainment to the voyager.

We found on this trip the same old amusements for passing away time that have prevailed for a score of years and more. The tossing of rope rings over an upright stake about ten feet distant from the pitcher; shuffleboard, or the thrusting of a sort of big checker or draught by means of a gigantic pudding-stick at a chalked-out diagram on the deck; and pitching pennies into a pint pot. In the smoking-room, the games of chess and checkers, whist, poker, and other games of cards, drew a strong representation from the male portion of the passengers, and caused a change of ownership of a very respectable number of sovereigns and bank-notes. Of course, the usual concert that is always given for that English Marine Orphan Asylum, that must be accumulating a handsome income from ocean-travellers by this time, took place on our voyage over; and the affair, being run by an English passenger, was conducted in true English style, by calling with some ceremony a titled Englishman to take "the chair."

Englishmen at a meeting, a private concert, and, I believe, at a sewing circle, if they ever had such an assemblage, always contrive to have some Sir Peregrine Poke or Lord Addington Adlehed on hand to "kindly consent to take the chair." Those who are present find that, besides having this fact reported in the newspapers or talked about in certain circles, the object of selecting such a chairman seems often to result in the obtaining of some one who can the most successfully muddle the whole affair.

The author recalls on one of his voyages, when we assembled to hear the amateur performance, vocal and instrumental, of several clever people who were on board, that the English gentleman who engineered the affair announced that "Sir Benjamin Baucher, K. C. B., had kindly consented to take the chair on this occasion," which the aforesaid Sir Benjamin, after being approached, did, looking quite red and uncomfortable. However, in a sort of beery bass, he explained the object of the charity, by aid of his prompter, and then proceeded to announce the performers set down in the programme, but, not having previously perused it, he announced some of the performers in the wrong places and mispronounced the names of the others. But the sea was smooth, passengers all well and in good-humor, the performances clever, and the usual toll taken up for the hospital was very respectable in amount.

It was a little bit of harmless exultation on our part to pass, just before entering Queenstown harbor, a steamer (the Britannic) that had left New York two days previous to our sailing, and to beat her in gaining port in such aggravating style.

The American Exchange in Europe, under the management of Mr. H. F. Gillig, is of great service to American travellers, and saves them a vast deal of trouble and annoyance. It has offices at London, Liverpool, Paris, and Berlin; and at each place, although somewhat of a seasoned tourist, I found its service to be of great advantage and at quite a small expense. At Liverpool its agent meets you as you disembark, has a carriage ready to convey you to rooms which you may have ordered in advance (as you should do, through him) at the hotel. You leave your keys with him at the landing, and he expeditiously gets your baggage through the Custom House, and saves a world of fussy annoyances that it is pleasant to avoid in your anxiety to exchange the bustle and confusion attendant upon landing for a "good square meal" on shore and a wide and steady bed in which to sleep.

There is nothing puts the life into one after the sea-voyage more than a good dinner after getting on shore, for it is without that indescribable ship-flavor, — half-way style of serving, lack of heat in vegetables, and other concomitants that characterize ship-cooking, — and is, of course, a more legitimate meal in all respects than those served on shipboard.

In a day or two, with digestive apparatus in good order, lungs filled with land-breezes, and sea-legs off, you are in condition to note the inferiority of English hotels in general, the great advantage possessed by the average American workman, employé, or day-laborer, over his English rival, in quickness of apprehension, in the adoption and use of an improvement, in the belief that anything may be improved, or that anything that is new can for any reason whatever be better than that which is old. In fact, the average Englishman seems to cling to the past, and look backwards, while the American is eager to leave even the present well enough for something in advance that may be an improvement.

Many of the American improvements now in use in England in machinery, manufactures, hotel-keeping, and travelling, though at first forced upon them and after long and persistent effort reluctantly adopted, now, after having come into common use, are claimed as English inventions.

Liverpool has changed but little since I saw it, seven

years ago; it has the same well paved streets, general seaport aspect in the business part of the city, and there is at the great hotels during the summer season that ever-changing rush of arrival and departure of American travellers by the great steamship lines. There through its streets is now laid the tramway or horse-railroad track, with double-storied cars crowded with passengers running over it. These tramway-tracks, it will be recollected, were torn up by the indignant people, and an injunction or something of the kind laid, twenty-five years ago, upon George Francis Train, to prevent his placing what was then called "this obstruction to public travel" in the street.

Train was clear-headed enough in those days; his only error of judgment was that he was fifteen years ahead of the average English intellect in appreciating an improvement in transportation. It was no novelty even then, for horse-railroads had been successfully running in America ten years previously. But in those days nothing American was thought to be of value; now, if a grand improvement is spoken of, a new invention referred to, or a superior article of goods exhibited, the first question asked by the English questioner is, "Is it American?" It is gratifying to find not only that articles bearing the American stamp now command the readiest attention in England, but also that many articles of American manufacture are displayed in the shop-windows, conspicuously labelled as such and competing successfully with similar goods of English make.

CHAPTER II.

ANY person that visited England a score or more years ago, and who goes there to-day, cannot fail to observe what enormous advance the United States has made in its manufactured products. In many of these we seem to have marched forward with giant strides, while our competitor has remained comparatively stationary; in other words, our protective tariff has enabled us to equal and rival him, as in the production of Bessemer-steel rails, or to outstrip him completely, as in the manufacture of watches.

Though I do not propose to write a tariff essay, I cannot leave the matter without alluding to the strong feeling that prevails, and which is gaining strength every day, against free trade in England.

The *Daily Telegraph* of London, a paper of very large circulation, published, in 1887, a series of letters from large and well known manufacturers, in various parts of England, calling attention to the fact that their business is being seriously injured, and in some cases ruined, by the influx of goods from some of the continental countries. Against these the labor, and the superior facilities of English manufacturers, could not compete, and some protection was called for against the free flooding of the English markets with foreign goods, and attention directed to the fact that, owing to the American tariff, that market was not only closed to them, but American manufactured goods were displacing theirs in British colonies. An ably edited weekly paper, entitled *Fair Trade*, published in London, was an outspoken opponent of English free trade as it then existed.

Our recently formed Protection League in New York has not yet, I believe, followed the example of the Cobden Club, and sent over pamphlets advocating the protective policy, to be distributed to voters on the eve of elections, or put up money prizes at England's educational schools for the best essays on the American Protective Tariff. Such a course might cause them over there to slowly consider the matter and to put a tariff upon American goods, perhaps by the time we get strong enough to manufacture all the goods England and the rest of the world wants, tariff or no tariff. Then how we should scold about England's Chinese wall and advocate freedom of trade in the admission of all American manufactured goods into British ports!

The change in the Liverpool hotels during the last twenty years has been great, although gradual. The fault-finding of Americans, their persistent demands, coupled with their readiness to pay liberally, seem to have had some little effect upon the English hotel-manager. He is gradually being forced to admit that he should try to conform to the demands, wishes, and desires of his patrons, and not endeavor to make them conform to his rules and regulations, even if such a course necessitates a departure from methods in use by his fathers before him, and now obsolete outside of his own island. The introduction of elevators and gas-lights into English hotels seems to have been fought with the most obstinate pertinacity, and is successfully opposed even now in several of the great hotels of London, as well as in York and other equally large cities in England. In like manner has the heating of halls or rooms by hot-air furnaces or steam been kept out to this day, to the positive discomfort of guests, as I can attest from my own experience during the raw, cold, and damp weather that prevails in London during the late fall season.

One obstacle to improvement in English hotels in large cities is the fact that they are owned by stock-companies, who manage them in that ponderous English way in which they conduct a coal-mine or cotton-mill, with a force of men, from manager down to boots and porter, acting under a set of cast-iron rules and regulations laid down by the board of directors, men of little or no experience, and with few ideas as regards the demands of a modern first-class hotel.

The clerical force of these houses is largely composed of men who do their duties mechanically, and simply serve their number of hours and then go off to their homes in the suburbs, giving place to their successors, and in turn take their places when their time comes round for them to return, but with apparently no sort of interest in what has been done or what arrangements made during their hours off duty, using no sort of judgment, and utterly careless and indifferent as to the convenience and comforts of the guest.

If any one desires to know the value of the bright, alert, well posted, and much abused American hotel clerk, let him sample a few of the ignoramuses that are placed in that position in the great London hotels. It was a notorious fact that pleasure-seeking Americans rushed over the ocean in such swarms at the close of our civil war as to completely crowd up all the London houses. Their demands for enlarged accommodations were such as to cause the erection of the Langham, Westminster Palace Hotel and others. The management of these English hotels was exasperating to the last degree to Americans, from the fact of their pretending so much and performing so little.

Large rooms and no gas-light, ignorant clerks and slow servants, a roundabout, slow-coach, and red-tape style of doing things, not at all in keeping with the quick despatch prevailing in America. The Langham Hotel at first became a resort for Americans. It had spacious drawing and smoking rooms, a fine dining-room, good *cuisine*, and was in a very desirable locality. Always full of Americans during the travelling season, the *attachés* had the impertinent independence to tell aggravated guests who complained of imperfect attendance, or who threatened to give up their rooms, that it made no difference — other Americans would be along to take them. And no special effort was made to please them or to cater to their tastes.

This, however, was several years ago. The influx of American travel and American dollars has continued, and it has dawned upon the sluggish British intellect that it would be best to encourage and not retard this influx; so new hotels, like the Metropole and Grand, were projected and built, and a third, still larger, is projected. The Langham no longer turns a cold shoulder to complaints, nor is it independent of American travellers, but actually advertises for them and solicits their patronage. "Think of that, Master Brooke!"

The two hotels in Liverpool most affected in 1887 by Americans were the Adelphi and Grand. The former is much improved and enlarged over the old-time affair; the greatest objection is that which attaches to most large English hotels, of contriving the entrances so that the lower halls and corridors are perfect sluiceways of cold, raw, and damp air, chilly and penetrating in early spring and fall, when Americans most frequent them. Then, in lieu of a warm, steam-heated drawing-room for guests, they provide a little, contracted, old-fashioned parlor, at one end of which is a fireplace containing two lumps of soft coal the size of brick-bats, that give out an enormous quantity of smoke and no heat, so that in cool weather, if you desire to keep warm in them, you must do as I did — wear your overcoat.

The great dining-room was heated (?) in a similar manner by a few lumps of coal in distant grates. This may have accounted for the action of two young Englishmen who came in one day and took a table near several others occupied by American ladies and gentlemen, and sat without removing their hats after ordering their dinner. This being observed by an American at one of the tables, he bade the waiter bring him an umbrella, which he immediately hoisted above his table. The other offenders against good manners took the hint and removed their hats, their act being followed by the immediate furling of the umbrella. At one of the Liverpool hotels the introduction of the "lift" or elevator was obstinately opposed, I understand, until a progressive stockholder agreed to put it in at his own expense.

Here we found the same exasperating English delay in responding to bells rung by guests. Chamber-maids for each floor, instead of bell-boys, attend to that service, or pretend to attend to it, for one to whom I gave an order at 10 P.M. went off duty, her time having arrived to do so, without telling her successor to fill my order, and, after waiting a long time for her return, her successor was by the second summons brought to give me that information and consume another fifteen minutes in executing the order, making the time in all about three-quarters of an hour to perform a service that would have been rendered in an American hotel in ten minutes at longest.

It really was not of much use to complain of such service (you are charged for it in your bill) to the woman occupying the little den, on the first floor, where the register and keys were kept, for she remarked that 10 P. M. was rather late for the order (it was for a pitcher of water) and the chamber-maid was probably tired! The manager — there is always a "manager" at these big English hotels, the title a misnomer from the fact that there appears to be no management in them — the manager comes out of his private office, smirks, smiles, and washes his hands with invisible soap, is quite indignant at our complaint, and begins at once to summon seven or eight chamber-maids, from various parts of the house, to account for the affair, creating an excitement and loud talk in the entrance-hall, from which we were only too glad to withdraw.

It is surprising that, in all these years in which Americans have visited London in swarms, there should not have been one great hotel built and managed upon the American plan, or that some of them should not change their cumbersome methods and adopt a few of the American customs in dealing with so large a proportion of guests of that nationality.

When the Grand Hotel in London was built, it was announced that such was to be the case, and English people who watched its large proportions when it was in course of erection gravely stated that it was to be a great Yankee caravansary, in which no English people would think of living. I noticed, however, during my stay that as large a proportion of English as Americans made use of it.

This house, which looks out upon one side of Trafalgar Square, is built upon a sort of semi-circular lot, and has the appearance of a large open fan. The rooms in the stories above the first floor are of that shape, the wider part of the room being at the two windows, the space narrowing off towards the door. If you have a fire in your sleeping-room, as I did, even in what is deemed a good-sized apartment it is so uncomfortably near the foot-board of the bed as to afford you the opportunity of shuffling off the mortal coil like John Rogers — with warm feet.

The annoyances here to Americans are many. Chief among them is the number of persons employed, and the gauntlet the guest must run to gain information, be served, or find any one who has the slightest knowledge of anything out of his individual department. Thus the man who receives your letters and room-keys is utterly ignorant respecting where a theatre is, at what hour its performance begins, or respecting the arrival or departure of any train from London. The man who assigns you a room can tell you the name of a good hotel in scarcely a town or city on the island, — and so on.

When I arrived at the Grand Hotel, in damp, dismal, cold November, the fresh-air or ventilating mania was prevailing as usual.

Arrived at the entrance of the house, the gilt-capped porter was at the cab-door to let me out; he summoned the house-porter to take my luggage; another porter, with gilt-striped pantaloons, opened the valve-doors, and held them open till I came in with my luggage, and admitted at the same time a full rush of chill wind into the lower hall, and through the opened doors, and into the great reception and reading room, containing numerous ladies and gentlemen. Next I went to the room-clerk, where names were registered. Great books of plans of the rooms were spread out upon desks and tables, and the office had the appearance of the headquarters of a major-general in active campaign.

My rooms had been engaged in advance, but it was now nine o'clock in the evening, and the day-clerk not on hand, and his successor, as usual, was oblivious respecting the matter, which had been arranged two days previously. Finally, after various explanations and the production of the day hotel-clerk's letter acknowledging that the apartments would be ready, some were assigned me. All this time the ladies of the party were out in the cold hall, by the main entrance, which the uniformed door-opener contrived to keep as uncomfortable as possible, by holding open the doors for those who wished egress or ingress, for a minute or two before they could possibly reach them. There was no more need for the fellow at the door than for a lightning-rod on a wash-tub.

The corridors and halls above the second floor were poorly lighted, and unheated; and made more chilly and uncomfortable in damp, foggy November weather by the windows being kept down at the top. Thus you step from the atmosphere of your room, made comfortable by a fire, out into entries and hallways with a difference of fifteen to twenty degrees of temperature.

The "lift," which carries you to the upper stories, is contrived with swinging doors, which the man who runs it is obliged to push open. He must also step out at every landing before the passenger can leave or enter. The automatic slide door, as was the case of the "lift" itself, will finally, after years of persuasion of the "board of direction," be probably solemnly voted in by them, at some regular meeting, where the motion will be duly made and seconded.

Besides the porter, or man outside the lower door to call cabs and receive guests, there were two more within, including the individual who opened the doors and acted as a sort of champion guest-cooler and pneumonia-promoter. Then, there was a luggage-porter in one corner; another, who received parcels for guests, in another; on the other side of the passage, a boy to change money and sell stamps, and further on the room-office, with the great plans and enormous bother of determining your rooms, requiring as much ceremony as if selecting an architectural plan for an eight-story mansion.

An inner office held the manager; next outside was a cashier, — of course, he knew nothing except how to receive money and receipt bills; then another small enclosure held two men, who kept the room-keys and letters; then the coat room; then, at the door of the great breakfast-room, stood a large, solemn, uniformed individual, whose sole duty was to bow when any one approached, and hold the door wide-open when any one went in or out the room, to the infinite annoyance of those inside, who were deluged with cold draughts of air, coming in from the other great doors opening into the street, held open by the other supernumerary.

All these men were scattered round so thickly, from the portal to the elevator, that you almost fell over them, and in attempting to get information of any kind you were referred from one ignoramus to another until driven to the verge of madness by the dense stupidity prevailing where you should find quick perception, certainly ordinary intelligence.

"But, then, the English are not an inquisitive people! They don't ask questions, like you Americans, and they have certain set customs, that it is hard for them to change," exclaimed a good-natured Briton to me.

It is not only that, but in the Anglo-American hotels they have great reluctance to depart in the least degree from a certain set of rules which they appear to have laid down, even if such departure is demanded by guests, and will contribute to their comfort. Complaint to any subordinate short of the manager, respecting an open window, a smoky chimney, an expiring fire in the public room, is treated with supreme indifference. The management evidently arranges the conduct of the establishment not with the idea that the hotel is to be managed to give the largest degree of satisfaction to the guests, but that the guests are to conform, in their comings, goings, and orders, to the satisfaction of the management.

"Please to shut that door!" said a shivering American to one of the head waiters in the dining-room, pointing to the open portal.

"Door, sir? yes, sir," and he hurried off in another direction.

The American rose from the breakfast-table and walked to the door, the swinging sides of which had been propped open, to save the great creature in gold-banded cap and breeches the trouble of opening and shutting them.

"Shut this door!"

"Er — I beg yer pardin?"

"Shut this door, it's too cold," said the speaker, kicking out the chocks, and letting the doors swing together.

"I beg yer pardin, but — er — the manager told me to keep' em hopen."

"How long ago?"

"Oh, months ago, sir."

"I thought so. Now I tell you to close them and keep them closed except when people desire to come in or go out, for I don't intend to freeze as well as starve while I'm here."

The doors were not, after this dialogue, propped open again.

The meals at these great hotels are: breakfast from 8 to 10:30; luncheon from 12:30 to 3, and dinner from 6 to 8:30.

The American who has been accustomed to the luxurious first-class hotels of New York, Boston, Philadelphia, Chicago, in fact any of the great cities of his own country, where abundance, variety, prompt service, and admirable *cuisine* are the rule, is simply astounded that there should be here, in the great metropolis of the world, such a comparatively meagre bill of fare, so little variety from day to day, and so close a calculation as to quantity served.

At breakfast he finds two kinds of fish, sole and whiting, and for hot meats perhaps steak with ham and eggs. The next day the fare was varied by leaving out the sole for another kind of fish and substituting chops for the steak, with the addition of sausages. As a favor, I got chops on the beefsteak day, after bribing the waiter,— the steak was one of the English sole-leather kind.

The thought of a Fifth Avenue Hotel breakfast bill of fare, beginning with fruit, grapes, oranges, pears, and including five or six kinds of fish, eggs in every known form of cooking, pork and mutton chops, lamb cutlets, broiled chicken, oysters, steak, potatoes in every form — but why go on? That breakfast bill of fare would drive an English hotel-keeper crazy, to say nothing of the *menu* for dinner.

Why, a Fifth Avenue Hotel dinner, if served in one of these London hotels at their rate of charge and their style of serving, would cost fifteen dollars a head and require ten hours between oysters and coffee.

Some of the courses at the Grand and Metropole were ludicrous in the extreme. Fancy being solemnly provided with a hot, clean plate, and, after waiting patiently till the dish reached you by the *table d'hôte* waiter, finding that the whole course was string-beans, and, the spoonful that you took being disposed of, you were next served with another course, say of lettuce or some other cheap grass stuff.

The great English hotels are very liberal in cheap greens, but economical in serving good roast solids that cost much. Who ever ate a good roast turkey dinner with cranberry jelly, mashed brown potatoes, celery, squash, sweet potatoes, macaroni, and three or four other side-dishes of appetizing vegetables in an English hotel?

CHAPTER III.

MUCH as the good living of England is vaunted, it cannot approach the American. Its principal staples are beef, mutton, and chops, ham (with eggs) for meats, sole and turbot for fish, sour gooseberry pie or raspberry tarts for "sweets," with a hunk of cheese and a few grapes by way of dessert, and, as an irate Yankee once said, the damnable frequency with which these are set before one at last makes one's very gorge rise with disgust at the sight. It will be understood that the author's criticism is chiefly levelled at hotels. For the sake of comparison, I give below the breakfast and dinner bills of fare of the Grand Hotel, London, and of the Fifth Avenue Hotel, of New York.

The Grand Hotel, London.

MENU DU DÉJEUNER.

FISH.

Fried Soles.   Fresh Herrings.   Finnan Haddock.

ENTRÉES.

Ham and Fried Eggs.   Scrambled Eggs aux Fines Herbes.
Stewed Kidneys and Mushrooms.
Home-made Sausages.   Mutton Chops.
Potatoes à la Maître d'Hôtel.

SUNDRIES.

Oatmeal Porridge.   Cold Viands.
Table d'Hôte Breakfast, consisting of Tea, Coffee, Cocoa, or Chocolate, including the Dishes mentioned above, 3s. 6d.

Fifth Avenue Hotel, New York.

BREAKFAST.

Fruit.   Radishes.   Cucumbers.

FISH.

Fried Codfish, with pork.   Salt Codfish, with cream.
Broiled Salt Mackerel.   Smoked Salmon.
Broiled Fresh Mackerel.   Fried Smelts.
Broiled Shad.   Hashed Fish.   Digby Herrings.   Fish-balls.

BROILED.

Beefsteak.   Mutton Chops.   Lamb Chops.
Veal Cutlet.   Pork Chops.   Ham.
Calf's Liver.   Pig's feet, breaded.   Pickled Tripe.
Mutton Kidneys.   Smoked Bacon.   Honey-comb Tripe.

FRIED.

Pig's Feet, breaded.   Oysters, with crumbs.
Pickled Tripe.   Calf's Liver.   Tripe, plain.   Clams.
Sausage.   Pork Chops.

STEWED.

Clams.   Mutton Kidneys.   Oysters.
Hashed Meat.   Hashed Chicken.

EGGS.

Omelets, plain, or with parsley, onions, ham, kidneys, or cheese, boiled, fried, scrambled, or dropped.

COLD MEATS.

POTATOES.

Hashed, with cream.   Lyonnaise.   Fried.   Baked.

BREAD.

Brown Bread.   Graham Bread.   Corn Bread.
Graham Muffins.   Rolls.   Rice Cakes.
English Muffins.   Oatmeal Mush.   Milk Cakes.
Plain Muffins.   Cracked Wheat.   Buckwheat Cakes.
Fried Indian Pudding.   Hominy.   Fried Hominy.
Dry and Dipped Toast.

Coffee, Chocolate; Oolong, Green, and English Breakfast Tea.

The Grand Hotel, London.

TABLE D'HÔTE DINNER.

POTAGES.
Consommé à la d'Orléans.   Crème à la Condorcet.

POISSONS.
Turbot à la Hollandaise.   Whitebait.

ENTRÉES.
Fontanges de Volaille Soufflées
Tournedos aux Champignons.

RELÉVES.
Saddle of Welsh Mutton.   Dindes à la Périgueux.

LÉGUMES.
Flageolets à la Maître d'Hôtel.   Pommes de Terre Noisettes.

RÔTI.
Bécasses sur Canapés.

ENTREMETS.
Abricots en Bellevue.   Cassolettes à la Duchesse.

DESSERT.
Glace Japonaise.   Fruits Assortis.

The reader will observe that a great deal of importance is given to the above by putting into French some very ordinary dishes. Especially is this done when "words of learned length and thundering sound" can be employed, as, for instance, those ignorant of the French language should know that "Flageolets à la Maître d'Hôtel" is not a musical-instrument dish, but haricot beans, cooked in the landlord's style; "Pommes de Terre Noisettes," simply signifies potato-balls, like hazel-nuts in size or color. Champignons is a grander-looking word for something to eat than mushrooms, and some of the other titles were incomprehensible until the production of the dishes they designated.

A friend who consulted his small pocket French dictionary, to ascertain the signification of "Cassolettes à la Duchesse," closed the book in disgust after finding the definition of the first word, which ran thus: "Cassolette, scent-box, perfuming-pan, odor, stench." The fact is that these French bills of fare, the world over, contain words that are coined from the brains of French cooks, and which cannot be found in the dictionary. They are often wrought into magnificent titles for the purpose of giving an insignificant production a grand designation. Putting the above all into plain English would have caused the list to have shrunk in importance to the uninitiated eye. Americans visiting London for the first time naturally expect to find hotel accommodations in that great city equal, if not superior, to their own, and their disappointment at the English style of management, and the impossibility of being served in the American style, has caused London hotel accommodation, or what Americans call the lack of it, to be one of the most prominent of the features of their European tour. Again, Americans are such frequenters of hotels in their transient visits to different cities in their own country, and so many are accustomed to make them a permanent abiding-place, that the subject is a familiar topic with them abroad. With these facts in view, the author has thought best to devote considerable space to the subject, in giving the result of his observations from an American point of view. For the sake of comparison, therefore, the dinner bill of fare at an American hotel is here given, in which the French titles are confined to "entrées" and even there so skilfully mixed with English terms as to leave little doubt as to their character in the mind of the unlettered guest: —

Fifth Avenue Hotel, New York.

DINNER.

Little Neck Clams.

SOUPS.

Chicken Gumbo. Tapioca.

FISH.

Boiled Kennebec Salmon, cream sauce.
Broiled Spanish Mackerel, parsley sauce.
Small Potatoes.

BOILED.

Leg of Mutton, caper sauce.   Corned beef and cabbage.
Turkey and Oysters.   Jole and Spinach.
Beef Tongue.   Ham.

COLD DISHES.

Beef Tongue.   Roast Beef.   Ham.   Boned Turkey.
Lobster, plain.   Chicken Salad.   Lamb.   Lobster Salad.

ENTRÉES.

Sweetbreads larded en macédoine.
Lamb Chops à l'Italienne.
Bouchées au Salpicon.
Croquettes of Green Turtle, anchovy sauce.
Macaroni à la Nicienne.
Cream Fritters à la vanille.

ROAST.

Capon.   Ham, Champagne sauce.   Mongrel Goose.
Beef.   Spring Lamb, mint sauce.   Turkey.

VEGETABLES.

Boiled Potatoes.   Onions.   Stewed Tomatoes.
Mashed Potatoes.   Bermuda Beets.   Baked Potatoes.
Rice.   Corn.   Turnips.
Green Peas.   Asparagus.

PASTRY.

Baked Cup Custard.
Rice Pudding.   Rhubarb Pie.
Apple Pie.   Lemon Kisses.
Jelly Puffs.   Almond Cake.
Charlotte Russe.

DESSERT.

Almonds.   Oranges.   Raisins.   Pecan Nuts.
Apples.   Strawberries.   Bananas.
Pineapple.   English Walnuts.
Vanilla Ice-cream.   Coffee.   Punch à la crème.

The style of charging dinners at the Metropole and Grand Hotel in London is to submit to you a printed blank upon which what you have ordered is written, and just before rising from the table you are desired to approve it by signature before the waiter carries it to the cashier to be charged to your account. If staying at the hotel for a few days you are only permitted to pay the bill on leaving, or, if remaining more than a week, at the end of each week, when the huge bill of items is handed in. It is of course impossible to tell then if the charges for the various meals have all been correctly posted from your order slip, unless one is blest with a memory not vouchsafed to ordinary mortals. A friend of the author who was staying there with his family made daily record of everything ordered in his pocket memoranda, by which he discovered errors of account necessitating an overhauling of thirty or forty order slips for the week.

"In future," said he to the book-keeper, "I will pay the waiter for each meal as I finish."

"Quite impossible, I assure yah, sir."

"Why so? I observe people do it every day."

"Er — yes, beg your pardon, but those are transients, sir."

"Well, consider me a transient and I'll pay as they do."

"Really! we couldn't! We — ah — 'ave to 'ave a system; — our enormous business, doncher know!"

"Enormous business! What do you call an enormous business?" said the now irate American.

"Why, immense dinner trade; why, we often have to dine two hundred and fifty persons a day hyar!" and the young man leaned back as if half expecting the American to reel under this announcement.

"How many!" said the latter.

"Two hundred and fifty a day!"

"Now look here, young man, don't ever tell that to any other American; if you do, he will laugh in your face for calling it a big business. Why, I am from a second-rate city where at one of our regular hotels from five to six hundred are dined daily, while three or four clubs of thirty to forty members each are having dinners in different parts of the house at the same time."

"Really? — most extwardinary!"

"Extraordinary! No, sir; I have sat down in a dining-room at Saratoga Springs where over a thousand were dined at once, with four times the variety to the bill of fare and with not half the trouble of getting served that there is in this country."

But why go on. The improvement over the small, stuffy, beer-saturated, antique, old-fashioned hotel of London thirty years ago is already so great that they are not now over twenty years behind us in America, and our sons and daughters in their visits twenty years hence to London will probably then find accommodations, regulations, and management up to to-day's American standard.

The reading and reception-room, or general sitting-room, as it might be called, at the Grand Hotel is very well supplied with English daily and weekly papers and magazines, among the latter two American ones. There was but one American newspaper, however, among the score or more journals upon the tables.

A large and well arranged public parlor and smaller writing-room are above-stairs for the convenience of guests. The managers of the great hotels here have not yet provided the convenient newspaper and periodical stand with attendant railroad and theatre ticket-offices within their halls.

Their whole minds are given to big dining-halls, committee-rooms, rooms for wedding-breakfasts or corporation dinners, grand vestibules, entrance-halls, liveried servants, and to forcing people to take suites—that is, a room and parlor—instead of single rooms. A man loses as much in an English hotel-keeper's esteem by taking but one room for himself and wife, and relying upon the public sitting-rooms, as he does by appearing in public in London or travelling about with any different kind of head-covering than a tall black hat.

The tyranny of the tall hat is such that the individual who presents himself at a banker's or should dare to call on a family at the West End in a soft or low-crowned hat of the American style, no matter how rainy the weather, would be looked upon askance and his respectability questioned until endorsed. Worse than that, no Englishman would dare go to church in any continental city in any head-gear except the regulation stovepipe. The comfort of the American soft hat must be foregone if you wish to be considered anybody among Englishmen. So let every American, as soon as convenient after landing in England, buy a good, heavy-timbered, well braced English hat and a leather fire-bucket hat-box to carry it in, both of which he will find to be badges of value at English hotels and in English company.

The public sitting-room or reception-room we have mentioned is the resort of ladies and gentlemen who come from distant points in the city or suburbs, dine at the house, and go to the theatre or opera in the evening. Here, for perhaps half an hour before starting, ladies would sit of a cold November day with their remarkably *décolleté* dresses, a wonder to us Americans at their hardihood and endurance as well as their apparent indifference at what seemed to some of us rather an immodest exposure.

"But," said a good-natured English friend, "we have, to be sure, chilly weather, but none of that tremendous cold that you have in America, necessitating the terrrible hot-air furnaces that we English cannot abide. Indeed, I have been brought up to live in a parlor where the temperature at the fireside was about 60° to 68° and other parts of the room not above 50° to 60°, and we prefer to endure a little cooler temperature than the 75° to 80° that prevails in your American houses and into which you are obliged to walk with the suit of clothes that you wear for an outside temperature of from only five to ten degrees above zero."

I confess there is something in this, but I observe these terribly *décolletée*-dressed women are troubled with bad colds. Influenza is prevalent. Upon asking a salesman who was suffering from it, in a store where I was making some purchases, why the door near which we stood was left wide-open, and if it could not be closed, on account of the chill air, he at once politely assented, with the remark, that he should be glad when it was two weeks later, as that was "the date ourselves and neighbors close the shop-doors, and put fires on."

Closed doors and fires probably would be refrained from till that date, even if the temperature had gone below the freezing-point, rather than break over an old and long established custom.

"Yes," said our English friend, "but you must remember that a country that has been a thousand years in existence gets into grooves, and has little else to do but to grow. You, with your cosmopolitan population, can and do take the best points of all nations and weld them into a fashion for yourselves — invent new fashions. With you novelty is the rule, with us conservatism. Educated here into certain habits and customs, under which we have got along very well generation after generation, you must admit it is natural for us to go slowly in adopting what has been foreign to our ideas of comfort and convenience."

There is some reason in this, and perhaps we Americans err in expecting the adoption of American fashions in England; but one thing is certain, I do not remember that any American travellers in England who have given their experiences have made more numerous and laughable blunders than Florence Marryat, in her book entitled "Tom Tiddler's Ground," which contains some ridiculous statements with regard to Americans, such as would convince one that she must have been thoroughly hoaxed by designing persons. Note the coarseness of the writer in alluding to the display of her arms and bust at her readings, at the length of her legs; and such expressions as the following: "As far as I am concerned, however, I never saw them (American ladies) drink anything but 'slops,' and I am afraid they must have been very much shocked at my brandies and sodas. But then I did all my drinking — not being ashamed of it — at the public table."

There is but little evidence in this, and other coarse vulgarities, that the author was or could be ashamed of anything, unless it might be lady-like courtesy and deportment. She remarks in the next paragraph in her book to the one above quoted: —

"With regard to American children, I am thankful to say I have seen but little. Doubtless they are as nice as most other people's brats, which is not saying much for them."

If the English people take, without any grains of salt, all the misrepresentations and collection of egotistic extravagancies that this Marryat woman presents in her book, as the truth about America, then we may not wonder that those who have not visited us should set their faces against anything said to be an improvement coming from this country.

Speaking of "The Truth about America," an Englishman named Edward Money, who travelled in this country for four months, recently published a book bearing that title, which is a collection of such outrageous blunders and falsehoods as to be veritably comic to the American reader, who, so far from being vexed at its glaring inaccuracies, can only roar with laughter as he reads page after page of its curious blunders, dense stupidity, and snobbishness.

Years ago, before English and Americans had made themselves so well acquainted with each other, we often heard of Americans who visited England being complimented upon the perfection with which they spoke English. Now the American discovers that there really is a difference in the language of the two countries. I do not refer to the cockney dialect of England, or the drawling, nasal tones of the burlesque Yankee, now so rapidly disappearing, nor the peculiar slang of the backwoods and frontiersmen, so often paraded as the genuine American every-day talk in English stories and English melodramas. As well might Americans cite Yorkshire, Lancashire, or Welch dialect as the every-day expressions and usual tongue of the average Englishman.

What at once attracts the attention of the newly

arrived American in English conversation is the rapidity of utterance and the upward inflection of the voice, which is the opposite to what he has been accustomed to. Indeed, I believe the sole cause of the failure of one of the most popular of London's comedians (Toole) in America was owing to the extreme rapidity of his utterance, rendering it difficult for the average American to follow him. But all Englismen are not rapid speakers. There is a class that

> "stick on conversation's burrs,
> And strew their pathway with those dreadful 'ers.'"

Some of our older readers will recall the performances of Mr. Macready, the eminent tragedian, which were criticised as marred by this habit in his most effective soliloquies and speeches, as for example: —

"Is this — er — a dagger that I — er — see before me, — er — the handle towards — er — my hand?"

Or: "To be — er — or — er — not to be — er — that is the question."

Then, there are different appellations given to the same things by Americans and English, but readily understood by both after a little experience, but, as an American once remarked, making the languages so different that we ought to claim our language for ourselves, and call it the American language and not the English.

The following glossary of a few well known terms and expressions will be readily recognized by those who have visited England: —

American.	English.
Immediately } Right away }	Directly.
Baggage	Luggage.

"AMERICAN" DRINKS.

Trunk	Box.
Ticket-office	Booking office.
Ticketed	Booked.
Elevator	Lift.
Conductor	Guard.
Driver	Coachman.
Engineer (locomotive)	Driver.
Fireman	Stoker.
Switched	Shunted.
Cars	Coaches.
Railroad	The line.
Rails	Metals.
Horse-railroad	Tramway.
Policeman	Bobby.
Boy	Lad.
Cane	Stick.
Uncomfortable / Unpleasant	Beastly.
Sick	Ill.
Twenty-five	Five-and-twenty.
Excuse me	Beg yer pardon.
A drink	A "go."
Overcoat	Topcoat.
Suspenders	Braces.
Overshoes	Goloshes.
Molasses	Treacle.
Pastry	Sweets.
Candy	Sweetstuff.
Powdered sugar	Castor sugar.
Rare	Underdone.

The popular idea of American drinks in London as paraded on programmes at some of the hotel and public bars seems to have been derived from the Western stories of Davy Crockett's time or the dime novel series of cow-boys and mining life. Perhaps the author has not been in the right locality in America, but certainly, in a pretty extensive series of rambles in his own country he has failed to find such titles for mixed drinks as Pick-me-up: Corpse Reviver, Buck-shot, Bull's Eye Hitter, Lay me out, Cock of the

Walk, Cowboy's Delight, Lightning Swizzle, Sherry Slap Up, Whiskey wake'em up. Why, in the name of all that is absurd it should be thought such appellations as these are American and would be attractive to Americans in London, none but the genius who contrived them can tell.

A couple of Americans had quite an amusing experience in one of the great public bars, where a conspicuous placard announced "American Drinks," and a small programme included the supposed attractive titles of American beverages above enumerated. Seating themselves at one of the small tables, the following dialogue took place between one of the Americans and the English waiter who came to serve them: —

"Do you have all kinds of American drinks here?"

"Certainly, sir. Everythink, sir. What'll you please to horder, sir?"

"Bring us two sherry chickens."

"Beg yer pardon, sir; we 'aven't any chicken, sir; would you 'ave a 'am sandwich?"

"Ham sandwich! No, I want nothing to eat! It's to drink — a couple of sherry chickens."

"Beg yer pardon, sir — must 'ave yer joke — but drinkin' chickens, yer know — can't *drink* chickens!"

"Look here, what are you talking about? Don't you keep American drinks here?"

"Yessir, certainly, sir."

"Well, sherry chicken is an American drink · go and get a couple of 'em — do you hear?"

"Yessir, certainly, sir"; and the waiter left with a look of mingled surprise and wonder on his countenance.

In a few moments the proprietor, a rotund individual in a bald head, mutton-chop whiskers, and white apron, appeared on the scene.

"Beg yer pardon, sir. Waiter made some mistake in his horder — did you want some sherry and a couple of chickens?"

"Nothing of the kind; we ordered some American drinks — a couple of sherry chickens."

"Sherry Chicken! Bless my 'art, sir, must be a new thing. We can give you Prairie Oyster, Corpse Reviver, Buckshot — but we 'aven't any of the chicken drinks."

"Why don't you keep some American drinks? You have a sign up."

"We do, sir; hall these are Hamerican, I assuah yer."

"Not a bit of it. I'm an American — been all over the country. My friend here has lived on a cattle-ranch and the frontier these five years, and never heard of these Corpse Revivers, and other absurd things you have here. Got any eggs?"

"Eggs? Yessir."

"Bring a couple and a pint of sherry, and I'll show you what a sherry chicken is."

The materials were brought, the yolks of two eggs dropped into two glasses of sherry, then thoroughly shaken together in the usual long glass used for that purpose, turned into clear glasses, and a dash of brown nutmeg thrown upon the foaming crest of the contents of each glass.

"There, sir, that's an American drink; that's a sherry chicken, and don't you forget it."

That the proprietor did not forget it, was proved by the fact of his having the next day prominently displayed a placard behind his bar, "Sherry Chickens." about the only title familiar to American eyes among the fanciful ones designating his other concoctions of liquid refreshments.

There are numerous small family-hotels in London where you can live comfortably and expensively, and, barring the hum and whirl of the busy travelling world, which the American learns to like and can enjoy without inconvenience at hotels in his own country; these lesser family-hotels are at present the most comfortable and best kept in London, because they are managed by one man or those who are individually interested in them, and not by a set of uninterested employés whose chief aim is to earn dividends for a syndicate or stock-company.

Indeed, lack of conveniences or comfort in English country inns can in no way be compared to those that exist in America. The horrors of some of the country hotels, even in our own New England, to say nothing of those at the West and South, must be experienced to be appreciated. England, however, in London and her other great cities, in the matter of hotels, ought to rival in comfort and convenience such cities as New York, Boston, Philadelphia, and Washington.

There is one thing to be said about the second and third rate hotels in England as compared with those in America. The latter are pitiful imitations in their bills of fare of the first class and one can rarely get anything good whatever at them, while the second or third rate English country inn, if it has nothing but eggs and bacon and ale, will generally have those of good quality.

CHAPTER IV.

The following communication was received by the author of these sketches: —

TREMONT HOUSE, June 13, 1887.

Sir: — This morning occurred the proudest moment of my life. About 7 A. M. I bade adieu to an exceedingly civil conductor and attendant, descended thankfully from an inconceivably stuffy car, and for the first time in a course of wanderings as devious if not quite as prolonged as those of the Aryan race, I placed my foot upon the Hub of the Universe.

A fly — a genuine British "fly" — quickly conveyed me to the hotel from which I date, the pleasantest, the most homelike, I have found on this side of the water, and I was soon ensconced in a quiet room overlooking a shady green. What happened next? Well, this. As an old member of the London press, I looked eagerly for the first Boston paper I could find. Thereupon the Commercial Bulletin not unnaturally presented itself, and the first thing that met my eye was an article on "English hotels."

Now, I am very far either from maintaining the perfection of the ordinary British hotel, or of denying the bona fides of your talented correspondent. In fact, though I have had experience of a good many of the principal hotels over here, as well as in London, Paris, Rome, Calcutta, and elsewhere, I have certainly avoided the American "caravansaries," as your correspondent calls them, which have grown up on English soil. For the attempt of the easy and the quiet-loving Englishman to imitate the rapid, restless, and rushing American always reminds me of the well known fable of the jackass and the terrier — make what you will out of the illustration; and I am quite contented with such old-fashioned comfort as may be encountered at the Grosvenor or the Great Western.

It is possible, therefore, that in the establishments to which your correspondent alludes there may be a special servant told off to open and shut a particular door, and a special order issued that that same door should always be kept open and never be shut at all; nay, it is even just conceivable that the obtaining of a mutton chop, in a hotel of that kind, may be a matter of favor, though I confess that to an Englishman that last statement appears rather "steep." But whatever truth or taste may dictate in regard to these matters, I venture respectfully to protest against your lending your influence to confound gluttony with gumption and gorging with gorgeousness.

Your correspondent complains because he had only a choice of two or three sorts of fish and the same number of dishes of meat; and I know there are American hotels which act upon the principle of the greatest gluttony for the greatest number. Nay, I have myself counted no less than seventy dishes upon a bill of breakfast fare — not one of them by the by betraying the slightest effort at any delicacy of dressing, and have been fitly rewarded by utter satiety before commencing the meal. But even here there are some hotels which recognize that temperance and moderation are an essential ingredient in eating no less than in drinking, and that to overload and embarrass the choice tends to pall and disgust the appetite very little less than overfeeding to destroy the stomach.

My breakfast here this morning consisted only of an excellent omelet and a beautifully cooked mackerel. My dinner this evening was just such as we might find at a first-rate English or French hotel — *no more and no less*. And if anybody is not satisfied with that, but wants the earth upon his bill of fare — well, let him go to Chicago. That is, I believe, the great place for feeding pigs.

I am, sir, your obedient servant,
AN ENGLISHMAN.

The author has, like the writer of the above, wandered somewhat at home and abroad, and his descriptions in these sketches are a record of actual experiences — no more, no less.

We are glad that the correspondent made the Tremont House his home in Boston. There he will be served far more promptly than at either the Grand, Metropole, or Great Western, as the author knows from personal experience. With regard to confounding "gluttony with gumption," our English visitor falls into the common error of many of his countrymen that guests are to go through an entire bill of fare such as furnished by the great hotels in this country.

In America the proprietors of the hotels in our great cities, recognizing that their hundreds of daily changing guests may, even from fastidiousness, have different tastes, provide viands in such variety that individuals may suit their especial taste.

Take, for instance, the bill of fare of the Fifth Avenue Hotel, published in the last chapter. In that the invalid (not glutton) may select from ten different kinds of bread, which are always ready for breakfast at five minutes' notice from 6 till 11 A. M. He may order oatmeal, cracked wheat, hominy, or Indian pudding, any one of which will be served him with equal promptitude.

At the English hotels we have mentioned only oatmeal was obtainable, and but bread, muffins or toast, the latter served, after long waiting, cold, in an invention admirably contrived to keep it so, and now out of date in this country, called a toast-rack.

The very best reply to the correspondent is that while the author has no intention of "confounding gumption with gluttony," yet in criticising the great English hotels he cannot subscribe to meanness as enterprise or complete lack of business tact in catering for the requirement of guests as a characteristic to be commended.

Our correspondent, who has evidently enjoyed the creature comforts of Chicago, naturally falls, Briton-like, into another error. Chicago is not the great place for "feeding pigs," but for slaughtering and disposing of them.

Singularly enough, the very next day after receiving the above letter came another, of quite a different character, from a well known New York merchant but just returned from London, whose comments upon the author's criticisms are in an entirely different vein, and more than endorse what has been set down in these pages. The following is his letter : —

NEW YORK, June 13, 1887.

I have read your letter on the English hotels, and it bringeth the tear to my eye. I have come back a victim to the infernal London Hotel Metropole, aided and abetted by its rivals in imbecility in France and Italy. I have got a bad case of rheumatism induced by the damp winds that search for you all over that house, and encouraged by a weak, anæmic state of the blood, which has been attained by an almost entire absence of food from the stomach. The Metropole coffee at breakfast, if persisted in for three days, will produce paralysis, and in a week utter imbecility, and the balance of the breakfast — *whew!* I once ordered a "filet steak," which it was agreed would be ready in half an hour; and at the appointed time we were ready, waited fifteen minutes more, got the alleged steak — which might have as well been veal for all we could tell — cooked to death and very *cold*.

I reached America alive only by the aid of an old restaurant up a back alley in the "city." It was called "The Salutation," and you were saluted with a steak or a chop cooked before your eyes in a manner that braced one up, and with a result — perfection. By this one meal a day I existed, and my wife, who is never hungry, existed on Metropole slop and by dining at private houses, which we did much of. Fine dinners, but in cold, damp dining-rooms, where drafts from unseen corners made merry with one's back hair. Well, I hope that I have escaped with my life. Three doctors have already experimented with my waterlogged condition, and a dentist has given valuable advice.

This fact should be impressed on all would-be travellers abroad: "A preparation of six months in an Avenue A boarding-house in New York, with meals in the basement, shady side, no fires (except for overcooking the food), and the lightest of clothing, is indispensable." If the patient lives through his preparation he can go, but let any one who has boarded at the Fifth Avenue Hotel understand that he taketh his life in his hand when he lands at Liverpool.

Yours truly,
MERCHANT.

What the average American misses sadly in many of the English country hotels is the lack of any visible improvement in their fittings, furniture, or appointments. Modern improvements seem to have been considered unworthy of adoption. This was brought strikingly to mind when, after a pleasant ride one day over the Eden Valley road, we arrived at the King's Head Hotel at Darlington, where it seemed as though we had stepped back into the year 1842.

The hotel here was a typical English inn. We descended from the coach and found no one to show us to any public sitting-room — there was none, except a commercial room and a tap-room, — and the ladies of the party stood in the draughty, chilly passage until I went back to the little den at the end of it, where landlady or bar-maid was installed with her pumps, liquor measures, etc., and made known my want of rooms, of course taking a private room for sitting accommodation and meals, in addition to bedrooms.

The furniture, fittings, bedding, and table-ware had evidently descended through successive ownerships or had done duty with successive landlords for more than half a century. There were the old pressed glass salt-cellars of my boyhood's days; old chairs and carpets whose very patterns bring back memories of designs that were popular four decades ago and out of which all the flush of youthfulness and feeling of comfort had long since been exhausted; candles to illuminate the close, stuffy rooms; beds that you had to climb into, and feather beds at that, down into the depths of which you slumped until brought up by the iron-like barrier of the antique mattress of straw or cotton beneath, that years of pressure had wrought into a couch of adamant; the cold linen sheets clung around you till your teeth chattered from the vain endeavor of your body to impart animal heat thereto in the cimmerian darkness that followed the extinguishing of the one or two feeble candles that had imperfectly lighted you to your couch.

"Well," said an American friend, "this is not nearly as bad as the hotel accommodations that you and I have had to put up with at the West in America."

"Very true, but there they had not been keeping hotels for nearly a thousand years."

Apropos of English travellers' mistakes, quite an amusing one is related of an English tourist who was finishing up a six weeks' tour in America. He was about to leave New York for Boston, where he was to take passage on one of the Cunard steamers, and was advised to start a day earlier in order to spend a day looking around Boston, of which he had heard much as a centre of literary culture and a beautiful city. This he decided to do, and in communicating the fact to a second friend later on, regretted that the steamer started so early in the morning of the day of sailing, necessitating his rising at six or going on board the night previous.

"Tell you how to manage that," said friend No. 2; "go to the Maverick House, which is quite near the steamer landing at East Boston, and you will save an hour or more in the morning of the day of sailing and be able to get your comfortable breakfast on shore."

The tourist cherished this advice, and, on arrival at the station in Boston late at night, bade the hack driver : —

"Take me to the Maverick Hotel, Boston, east, please."

"Oh! you mean Maverick House, East Boston, I s'pose."

"Quite near the English steamer the place is."

"All right, sir! jump in!" and the passenger got into the carriage, leaned back and dozed over what appeared a long ride, crossing a ferry, and finally bringing up at a hotel where he was received and bestowed for the night.

Next morning, after breakfast, he prepared for a stroll around Boston, and asked a lounger near the door what there was "worth seeing hyar."

"Nothin' but docks," was the reply of the party interrogated, as he withdrew his cigar to expectorate.

The tourist passed out, and returned in two or three hours, dust-covered and disgusted, when he remembered that he had heard much of Boston's beautiful suburbs, so, after refreshing himself, he applied to the host to obtain him a carriage for a pleasant drive in the country.

The vehicle was duly provided and the traveller again set out. He returned in a pet, and departed early next morning with sundry expressions of disgust at the attractions of Boston and the rates of carriage-fare in that city.

Among those to whom he related his experiences on his return was a well known citizen of Boston, who expressed surprise at the denunciations of the traveller.

"Very dusty, cheap city, no public buildings of any note, principally a mere shipping and workshop town. Was told to see the docks. Docks! They call old wooden piers there docks. Many of the streets unpaved. Only one good hotel."

"What is that?" said the American. "Why, where did you stay?"

"Maverick Hotel, sir."

"Why, that is in *East* Boston, across the water, and not the city proper."

"Eh? Ah, yas; Boston, east; went there to be near steamship, you know."

"But were you never in Boston before, and did you not go over the ferry?"

"Ferry! Oh, yas, went over that late at night, when I arrived."

"And you did not go back over it next day?"

"Bless me, no! I supposed that was the outskirts and business part of Boston. No use seeing that, you know."

"Well, you spoke of an afternoon ride to the suburbs."

"Oh, ah, yas; blarsted humbug — Boston suburbs. Coachman took me to a place called Chelsea; no 'ospital like ours, nothing to see. Boston docks — another humbug; why, there's not a bit of stone like we have in Liverpool. And then the streets and churches and all that sort of thing, you know; beastly place — great disappointment, I assuah yar."

Even after the American had taken pains to convince the traveller of his mistake in having seen but a small portion of the city, divided from the more populous and attractive portion by water, and devoted chiefly to wharves, factories, railroads, and machinists' shops, and that in so doing he had entirely missed seeing the real metropolis of New England, the latter was hardly convinced, and wondered how men of literary tastes could live among so much dust and confusion.

English shops the author has fully described in former volumes, but this bit of advice may be given, that those who parade as butchers, bakers, or candlestick-makers "to the Queen," "His Royal Highness the Prince of Wales," or any of the royal family, generally charge you a shilling or two more than you pay for the same articles elsewhere, and have a stock that is limited in variety. Then, there is that provoking charge, "a guinea," a coin that you never see except in a numismatic collection. The guinea charge is used by fashionable physicians and swell jewelry, china, print, and book stores as an excuse for getting an extra shilling on each pound sterling charged.

I recall a young dealer in rare books and prints that I used to visit ten or a dozen years ago, in an odd, old-fashioned store at the corner of an alley in London, whose tumbled-together merchandise on crammed shelves in his little shop was a delight to bibliomaniac or bibliophile to overhaul. One could pick up choice bits, too, at a fair price. There were ragged pamphlets that one might buy for threepence, and choice old black-letter tomes for ten pounds. Books for a shilling and books for a sovereign; volumes for "three pun' ten" and a concession made you for a round lot. But one day a friend saw more money in the business, joined him in partnership, put in a good bit of capital, and wisely moved up into a good, aristocratic neighborhood. The shop, with its plate-glass windows and dark shelves with richly bound books carefully arranged, was eminently respectable, not to say aristocratic, and literary "swells" were induced to patronize it.

When I visited my former acquaintance some years after this successful move had been made, I was struck by the different style of my reception than that of former days. Then it was, "This is a nice copy of the book, price only sixteen shillings"; or, "Here is one, with worn binding, you can have for seven shillings, and put any binding on you fancy"; "Very good copy, this, three pounds, and well worth it too, sir. Look on that shelf, sir; there you will find some bargains from an auction sale last week. This little volume, with damaged cover, only three shillings."

Now, at this later day, as I entered, I found choice old illustrated books had been put into sumptuous bindings. Regiments of old friends shone in new uniforms — rare specimens of old tomes in clean and perfect condition astonished the book-buyer, and, it may be said, so did the prices. The dealer had good specimens, and was bound to have good prices. No worn-out covers or ragged tomes for you to buy cheap, and furbish up at the binder's. The old stock, what there was of it, was carefully stowed out of the way, at the rear of the store, and the choice specimens were wisely kept on view in front.

Recognizing bibliomaniacs or bibliophiles at once, the dealer never molested them as they entered, and pulled down volume after volume in their explorations, but wisely occupied himself at some little distance away, making no sign or remark that he noted their presence, until spoken to. Then it was they found that choice stock, store, and surroundings were to be paid for by the guinea exaction.

"What is the price of this?"

"Four guinass."

"How much for these?"

"Six guinass."

"And this little book?"

"One guinaa."

"Confound it, man! do you not sell anything here for pounds, shillings, and pence?"

"Beg yer pardon, nothing for pence, yer know; rarely anything for less than 'arf a guinaa — hurt our trade hyar."

The merchandise was rare, choice, well cared for; but the charm of the fusty, musty old literary mine was gone, and, with a sigh, the wandering book-lover turned away in search of some place where he might dig, delve, and exhume for himself some literary rarity, and, after purchasing, gloat over it by right of discovery. But the old opportunity of picking up rare books for a trifle has passed. Nearly every dealer, large and small, owing to the largely increased demand, is now well posted as to the value of rare and scarce books. There is this difference in a shop like the one above mentioned to others, and that is, one will have to pay guineas instead of pounds for his purchases.

CHAPTER V.

A SHORT ride from Darlington, and we were at Ripon, where the great cathedral and the beautiful ruins of Fountains Abbey are the historic sights that will claim the attention and interest of the tourist. The city of Ripon is in the county of York, and nearly midway between London and Edinburgh, being two hundred and twelve miles from the former, and one hundred and ninety-one from the latter city. It stands on a slight eminence, which gradually rises from the two little rivers Yore and Skell, and over the Yore is one of those beautiful English bridges, built entirely of stone, with graceful arches, seventeen in number, supporting its two hundred and sixty yards of length.

Of course Ripon is one of those old English towns that have many antiquities, and much history to interest the student and antiquarian, and dates back to the seventh century, the grant of lands for the foundation of a monastery being made, it is said, in 660. The site of Fountains Abbey, however, according to local history, was granted in 1132 by Thurstan, Archbishop of York, out of his liberty of Ripon, to certain monks who had separated themselves from what they deemed the lax discipline of the Benedictine Abbey of St. Mary in York, and it became in time one of the richest and most important monasteries in England.

A pleasant day renders a drive in the country in England doubly enjoyable, and such we enjoyed as we rolled over the smooth, well kept roads, amid English rustic scenery, until we reached the entrance to Studley Park, where we descended for our walk of about a mile to the ruined abbey.

The grounds of Fountains Abbey are owned by the Marquis of Ripon, and are magnificent in extent and in exquisite landscape effects. Lofty, luxuriant trees are there, and closely shaven lawns, evergreens of stately growth, and gigantic beech-trees that throw a grateful shade over the well kept driveway, which leads one along past shelving crags or beside a swift-flowing stream, the banks of which are adorned with statues and fountains. Pathways and rambles lead up over the steep embankments, and in the dense hedges, ever and anon, are openings through which the most lovely stretches of scenery are obtained. A little temple crowns an elevated point from which a beautiful panoramic view is had, and a view through a great opening in the foliage made by pulling aside a sliding door is indeed a "Surprise," as its name indicates. It shows a great reach of scenery, which appears as if especially laid out for the view, as, doubtless, much of it was, forming one of the most charming landscape effects I ever looked upon. But on the regular, broad walk we soon caught sight of the abbey as we approached it. In every respect it was the picturesque old ruin that one reads of in song, legend, and story — the lofty Gothic entrance, tall, Gothic window, square tower, and long stretch of ancient walls with their green mantle of ivy swaying in the summer breeze.

The tall tower of the abbey, at the end of the north transept, we were told, was 168 feet in height, although not appearing so high as we stood within the area of its base, which covers about twenty-five feet. Of course, the floors of its several chambers, glass of its windows, and the ornamental pinnacles have fallen, but the great, square, massive walls of masonry are solid as ever, and far up on each of the four sides are ancient Old English inscriptions interspersed with the carved arms of the abbey, three horse-shoes, mitre and keys, figures holding shields and palm-branches, and other devices.

Then we wandered through the whole of this beautiful ruin, which is kept clear of rubbish, and convenient for visitors, and with all that can be preserved as much in the original form as possible.

There was the old choir with its aisles of elegant design; the nave, which one sees at its best on entering the great western door, giving impressive effect with its massive columns 23 feet high and 16 feet in circumference, without a triforium intervening between them and the plain splayed windows above; the transept with its supporting arches of Norman architecture. The eastern transept is about one hundred and fifty feet long, and has a great east window of Gothic architecture. The cloister court, a great area of 128 feet square, is still surrounded by the buildings of the monastery; two sides of this were occupied by the monks, where they studied, and were also used for the instruction of novices.

The ruins of the chapter-house show it to have been a splendid hall in its day. Its dimensions are 85 feet long by 41 feet in width. There were ten round marble columns, the ruins of which still remain, which divided this hall into three aisles. The remains of a triple tier of stone seats are pointed out as those occupied by the monks when they assembled here for deliberation. According to the old Cistercian rule, abbots should be buried in the chapter-house, and the curious visitor may here find several stone coffins that have been exhumed, and interest himself in trying to decipher the rudely sculptured Latin inscriptions upon the slabs that formerly were set in the flooring. We were shown the seat said to have been occupied by John de Cancia in presiding as tenth abbot of the monastery for over twenty years (from about 1220 to 1240), and directly beneath it the memorial slab that was placed over his grave.

On another side we were shown the remains of the lay brethren's dormitories, refectory, buttery, kitchen, lavatory, etc., till it seemed like inspecting the ruins of a magnificent hotel of the olden time, where every creature-comfort that could have been devised for the occupants was provided. Even the lavatories were splendidly drained by water running beneath their sixty-foot hall. The refectory was originally a splendid room, about one hundred and ten feet by fifty, and the buttery is a curiously contrived room opening into it, in which are still remains of a stone drain, boiler, and lead piping.

At one side of the building used as a kitchen was a huge heap of ashes and other rubbish that had been cast out of a back window. This was dug over a few years ago to see if any relics could be discovered. Amid the oyster and mussel shells, with here and there beef and venison bones, were discovered a curious old silver spoon, coarse antique smashed jugs, ornaments evidently broken off silver plate, and other articles of trifling value, but interesting as connecting the monastic life in which they figured centuries ago with that of to-day, as the curious delver exhumed them from where they had been cast by careless hands of olden time, much after the same manner as characterizes the servants of to-day.

Nor were the provisions for sickness neglected, as we were shown in the ruins of the infirmary and the Great Hall, as it is called, connected with it. This must have been a magnificent apartment, for it was 171 feet by 70, and the roof was supported by eighteen cylindrical columns, the bases shafted and banded with marble, the positions of which show that it was divided into a nave and two aisles. All these cloisters, church, halls, infirmary, etc., are reached by connecting passages, it should be borne in mind, for this monastery, in its prime, was one of the richest in the kingdom, and these ruins cover many acres of ground, while the ancient boundaries of St. Wilfred of Ripon were an uninterrupted space of thirty miles.

But I will not attempt descriptions of cloisters, granaries, chapels, chapter-houses, and the vast range of various buildings used for this truly regal residence of the monks that inhabited them in this charming and fertile part of the country. The abbey was one of the grandest and most complete monastic residences of its times, as its ruins and history attest, and, being favored by popes, prelates, and kings with various immunities and privileges, enriched by a succession of princely gifts and the purchase of sepulture within its walls by large donations of money from persons of opulence and rank, it was an institution of no mean power in the kingdom.

It certainly is one of the most extensive and picturesque ruins in England, and one that will fully come up to the imagination of those who have only read of ruined abbeys and castles.

Before leaving Ripon, we visited the cathedral. It

was in the afternoon, when a service was being held, in which the cathedral choirs of Ripon, York, and Durham united in rendering the vocal portion of the service. This was superbly given, and the beautiful soprano and alto of the boy vocalists, combined with several magnificent bass singers (men), sent a flood of melody through the great building, that made its arches ring with glorious harmony.

The ancient name of Ripon was Inrhypum, and the foundation of this church was a Benedictine monastery. St. Wilfred, who appears to be the patron saint, I find, on looking up his history, was an abbot before A. D. 661, and some accounts say that he was the founder of this religious establishment.

One of the chief benefactors of the monastery at Ripon was King Athelstan, who made it a sanctuary, and extended the privileges of it a mile from the town in all directions. He who violated it was liable to lose both life and property. The boundary of this sanctuary was marked by eight crosses, at the close of the thirteenth century, called mile crosses; the positions of three are still indicated. The present cathedral dates from the twelfth to the fourteenth century, and, although not so large and imposing as others in England, yet is a stately edifice of grand proportions.

The north-west front, by which we entered, has two tall, square towers, with a pointed gable between. The entrance was through one central portal and two each side of it, all of pointed Gothic architecture, and above were three divisions, each with its tall pointed windows filled with stained glass. We could get but an imperfect view of the interior, as service was going on. A richly carved stone screen — a perfect mass of carving, nineteen feet high, on which are represented the

Deity and angels — separates the choir from the transept. There are lofty and graceful arches on each side of the choir, supported by clustered columns.

The great east window is a superb piece of stained-glass work. Its different decorations contain the coats-of-arms of different benefactors of the church. It was placed there in 1854, at a cost of £1000. The carving of the wood-work of some of the stalls of the dean, prebendaries, and other church officials is beautifully done, and on a portion of the wood-work the date of 1494 was pointed out to us. From the centre of the choir the view is beautiful and impressive. One should look first to the east end, which terminates with the great Gothic window, and then to the west end, where, within another great Gothic arch, jut out the decorated pipes of the organ, below which are the carved and ornamented canopies of the stalls, and on the sides the open pointed arches.

There are very few monuments in this cathedral; the most remarkable is of marble, and in the nave, on which is rudely sculptured a man kneeling and a lion. It is said to represent an Irish prince and knight who was buried here, who returned from one of the Crusades bringing with him a lion that followed him about like a dog.

The length of this cathedral (interior) is 266 feet from east to west. The nave is 167 feet and the choir 101. The breadth of the nave and aisles is 87 feet. The transept is 132 feet long by about thirty-five broad, and the height of the towers is 110 feet. The people of Ripon boast that their cathedral, although it may not be the largest, is one of the best proportioned churches in the kingdom.

In the big, square market-place is a monument,

nearly a hundred feet in height, erected to William Aislaby, who represented the borough for sixty years in Parliament. Most of the streets are narrow, like those of other ancient English towns.

It will be recollected, by those who have read the history of Robin Hood, that it was the " Curtall Friar of Fountains Abbey " with whom the merry outlaw had an adventure in crossing the stream, each compelling the other to carry him across the little river Skell until the Friar ended by throwing Robin into the stream. During a bout that followed between the two, Robin Hood, with his bugle-horn, summoned a score of bow-men, while the Friar, with a silver whistle, summoned a pack of fierce hounds. A truce followed, and the Curtall Friar (Tuck) and Robin struck hands, and became friends.

The romantic dale near the river, as you approach the abbey, seems a fitting spot for the scene of Robin Hood's romances, and you are shown " Robin Hood's Well," near a green knoll, as proof positive that this was the scene of some of the bold outlaw's exploits.

And this was " in ye oldenne tyme." Indeed it was; and, when the author was at Ripon, preparations were in progress for celebrating the thousandth anniversary of that city's civic life.

Only think of this! We juveniles who have recently been pluming ourselves in this country on our centennials! There was a city about to celebrate the millenary festival of its civic life! This celebration was to include a grand procession, in which Robin Hood and his men, including Friar Tuck and Allen a Dale, were to figure, as well as other historic personages of the past. Special service was to be held at the cathedral, where the Archbishop of York was to preach; a grand luncheon to be given in the public market-place, the festivities of the first day winding up with a torch-light procession.

The three days' public festivities began August 25, 1886. The houses and market-places were all gayly decorated. Venetian masts held long streamers and festoons of flowers, and great wreaths twined about them. The motto of the city was conspicuously displayed: —

"Except the Lord keep the city, the watchman waketh but in vain."

The public buildings were all decorated with flags and streamers. The bishops of Chester and Durham and the mayors of Darlington and Stockton took part in the proceedings.

The first day was delightful as to weather, and the reception of dignitaries, the procession of yeomanry escorting visiting mayors and other officials, in purple, black, and scarlet robes, the mayors wearing those huge chains of office and having great maces borne before them, was a feature of the day.

At the cathedral, the choir sang a modern version of a processional hymn written by King Alfred, to a tune taken from a MS. of the thirteenth century. A grand public luncheon was then given, of which twelve hundred people partook, but the feature of the day was the antique procession and old English "revels."

The master of the revels, clad in an Elizabethan dress of old-gold velvet, with a train of cloth-of-gold embossed with figures of animals, ships, and birds, read a proclamation at the market-cross, stating the revels should begin that night. He was surrounded by his pages, chamberlains, and marshals, all dressed in quaint old English costumes. After this proclamation a most grotesque procession paraded the streets. There was an advance-guard of boy dogs, a band of dancing satyrs and ogres, a cavalry band of men in hobby-horses, a band of huge brewers with a great car of beer-casks (what would any celebration in England be without beer?), then millers, cloth-workers, and other trades, not forgetting the makers of the celebrated Ripon spurs. The various civic dignitaries brought up the rear, the procession and streets being illuminated by bands of torch-bearers.

The grand affair, however, was on the last of the three days, the 27th of August, when a procession representing England in the olden time marched through the streets of Ripon and on through the beautiful grounds of Fountains Abbey lent for the occasion by the Marquis of Ripon. The route of the march was along the borders of the beautiful sheet of water which extends through the grounds out and in along the broad walk under the grand old trees. It was an effective and beautiful pageant. There were Druids with their oak-crowns, white robes, and long staffs, and arch-Druids with their golden sickles, — bards with long flowing beards and their golden harps, the jester in his blue and white silk motley and cap and bells, — the Emperor Hadrian in his Roman chariot, guarded by a whole troop of Roman soldiers in brazen helmets, crimson tunics, and shining greaves and breastplates.

The huge boat of the Viking, with its crew, the sides of the boat hung with shields, and the boat itself filled with the wild, shaggy-bearded Norsemen, grasping their gleaming weapons; the old Ripon abbot and Prince Alefrid in Saxon costume, various Saxon kings and queens in their chariots, surrounded by attendants in the costume of the period. King Athelstane, Archbishop Odo and a train of monks, King Henry IV. and his queen, and a troop of Norman knights who visited Ripon to escape the plague that raged in London during their time.

Robin Hood and a whole troop of his merry men in Lincoln Green, with cloth yard shafts and long-bows, St. Wilfrid and a troop draped in white and crimson and bearing shields, arms, and emblems of the ancient kings of Northumbria; King Alfred, strong and stalwart, with the standard bearing the emblem of the old Saxon Horse; May-pole dancers, shepherds and shepherdesses, harvest queens and hobby-horse riders. The whole formed a wonderfully curious and admirably costumed set of characters, in a procession over a mile in length.

The play of Robin Hood and the Curtall Friar was enacted, a grand luncheon served to the characters of the procession in the cloisters of the abbey, a tournament of knights on hobby-horses held in the tilting-ground, tilting at the quintain and ring, archery, single-stick, quarter-staff, and other old English sports were indulged in, and altogether the three days of revel and jollity were thoroughly enjoyed.

Really Ripon could have celebrated the thousandth anniversary of its distinct historical existence two hundred years ago, for the life of the town extends far beyond a thousand years. It was a thousand years ago that Doomsday Book was compiled, and the original abbey prior to Fountains was then a heap of ruins. Three hundred years before William the Conqueror's time the King of Northumbria presented the monastery and adjacent land to Wilfred, who, on becoming Archbishop of York, erected Fountains.

A thousand years of civic life, however, may be reckoned as something more than respectable antiquity. There were honest, steady-working folks in Ripon, in the very infancy of the feudal system, when there was not a king's justicer going circuit in England, and when the crime of murder might be purged by a money payment. Ripon tradesmen were weaving at their looms and measuring their cloth when the news reached them of the first Crusade, and doubtless many of her sturdy sons joined in that expedition. Ripon was a thriving and busy place before Ireland was conquered, Wales subdued, or Magna Charta signed at Runnymede, and its men fought gallantly at the battles of Crecy and Poictiers. The Scots ravaged the place in 1319, the Parliamentary troops, like vandal Puritans as they were, sacked the minster in 1643, and various other historic events figure in the life of the ancient city. Truly it seems *old* England, indeed, to us of "states unborn in ancient lore," when we begin to search the musty chronicles of the lives of her ancient towns and cities.

CHAPTER VI.

FURNESS ABBEY.

A RUIN second only to Fountains Abbey in extent is Furness Abbey, which the tourist should not fail to visit during his trip through the English lake country. The author took train from Liverpool at about 10 A. M., *via* Preston and Lancaster, for Windemere.

It is a beautiful ride by the west margin of Derwentwater, Borrowdale, through a valley six miles long watered by the river Grange, — a stretch of lovely English scenery; Grange appeared to be a lovely seaside place with Park Hotel and lovely cottages and villas.

We whirled past Ulverston and Lancaster and the celebrated Seven-Mile Sands, the railway track passing near the very edge of them for three or four miles, and we had an excellent opportunity of seeing this remarkable expanse, which is nothing more nor less than a wide estuary between Lancaster and Furness, which has been filled up by two rivers with mud and fine sand.

When the tide of the sea is out, the sand-bed is laid bare for a mile or more from shore, and its smooth, sandy surface may be crossed by a coach and four at quite a distance from shore. We passed when the tide was out and vehicles could traverse without difficulty; a few hours later and several feet of water covered the widely spreading sandy expanse, with vessels sailing where the stage-coach and wagons had been.

About six miles from Ulverston our train pulled up at Furness, where we debarked to remain a short time and visit the ruins of the abbey. The rush and rattle of the railroad train seemed almost a profanation of this beautiful and sheltered glen, so well adapted for a quiet old abbey, where its sandalled monks might enjoy all that was soothing and beautiful in nature. for their abbey was charmingly situated in the lap of an exquisite little glen watered by a little river which flowed through it.

Formerly, the great forests spread over the surrounding country, and it would have been difficult to have found a more secluded spot. The surroundings now render the fine old ruins all that one would imagine as picturesque; the rich verdure around contrasting with the grand old arches of crumbling red stone, and the masses of ivy upon its walls festooning them like vast curtains of living green.

The abbey was founded in 1127, by Stephen, afterwards king of England, and richly endowed by him. The abbot of Furness was a sort of king himself in his domain, which covered quite an extent of territory in the vicinity, and neighboring proprietors were glad to retain his favor by gifts, and his military powers in defence of their estates against Border tribes or other outlaws, from whose incursions or depredations they were likely to suffer; for certain Norman nobles, to whom lands had also been granted in the vicinity, came with the monks, and tributary herdsmen, with their flocks, settled down over these verdant slopes.

The lords' lands were divided into tenements, and each tenement, besides paying a proper rent, was to furnish an armed man to be always ready for battle when called upon. Each tenement was divided into four portions, and each portion held by an emancipated serf, one of the number being always in readiness for defence or to go to the wars. Shepherds, also, by permission of the abbot, made enclosures about their huts for their flocks, and these people all availed themselves of the religious privileges and influence of the institution, besides paying tribute to it in one way or another.

The abbots maintained quite a small army, numbering twelve hundred able-bodied men, and exercised as supreme power in Furness as the rulers of a principality. Their revenue, in the time of Edward I., was equal to nearly a hundred thousand dollars of our money per annum, which is some indication of the wealth of the institution.

The monks that inhabited this abbey were Benedictines, called "gray monks," from the color of their habits. After some years, they were changed to the Cistercian order, to which they belonged at the time the abbey was given up and abandoned, in 1537, four hundred and thirteen years after its first establishment. It contained, at the time of its dissolution, thirty-three monks and one hundred lay brethren. The monks consisted of two distinct classes: the clerical, who attended the choir, and were wholly devoted to religious duties; and the lay brethren, who tilled the land and performed the servile work of the monastery. The latter were treated the same as the former, except not being allowed the use of wine.

The abbey property, after passing through various hands, finally came into the possession of the present owner, the Duke of Devonshire. The grounds are kept in good order, and the owner allows free ingress to all parts of the ruins, which extend through a vast extent of park. A wall enclosed the church and other structures, while a second wall enclosed the old fishponds and a park of about eighty-four acres.

We had not walked a dozen yards from the little railway station before we stumbled over the base of ruined pillars half-buried in the earth, the remains of the abbot's chapel and some forgotten out-buildings; and, as we pass on, there is a comfortable hotel, built on the site of the abbot's house. A short distance further on, by the public road at the rear of the hotel, we find this beautiful dell bears the somewhat startling name of "Valley of the Deadly Nightshade." The mouldering walls, roofless church, and outlines of buildings still visible, show what a huge religious house Furness Abbey must have been in its time. There is a charm in the still exquisite designs of even the ruins of these old abbeys of England, that makes one love to linger among them in silent admiration of their graceful and picturesque proportions.

The north entrance to the transept, through which I passed, was a high-arched Norman door-way; above it was the open space of what was once a huge, magnificent Gothic window, and in the wall that stretched away at one side, other narrower windows, with pointed Gothic arches. It is difficult, without the use of plans or engravings, to give the reader a correct idea of the extent of these old abbeys or the magnificence of their proportions, for they were vast religious palaces with their churches, guest-halls, chapels, infirmaries, cloisters, chapter-houses, dormitories, and kitchens. Fill up these gracefully arched windows with stained glass, once more crown the walls with lofty roof, replace the fallen pillars and clustered columns in erect position, and restore the lofty towers, the beautiful carvings and decorations of the great nave and transept, and sur-round all with gentle slopes, grand park, winding river, and well stocked fish-pond, and it must have been a paradise to have enjoyed a life of peace in, rather than a place to retire from the world as an act of duty or penance.

But even now, as we enter the grass-grown enclosure of the roofless church, we obtain some idea of what it must have been in its prime, from its present condition; for the walls, with the exception of the north one, are in good preservation.

The church is 304 feet long and 66 feet wide. The nave had alternate clustered and solid pillars. The transept is 129 feet long and the walls massive, being from four to six feet in thickness. The chancel is sixty feet long from the transept, and here at one end of it is the magnificent east window, which now is but a great opening 47 feet high and 23 feet broad. Fortunately, the glass, which is a superb specimen of the stained glass of the Middle Ages, was carefully removed after the abbey was given up, and it is now placed in the church at Bowness.

There are two other great windows in this chancel, each forty feet in height. The grand altar was situated immediately under the east window, and at the right of it still remain the sedalia or seats occupied by the white-robed officiating priests during the ceremony of high-mass. These are separated from each other by richly carved stone-work, and above them is a canopy, also of elegant work of the sculptor's chisel. From the south transept, you obtain access by a stone staircase to the dormitory, from which one may look down into what was once the refectory, where the abbot and monks of old assembled to discuss creature-comforts at their bounteous board: —

> "And the abbot meek,
> With his form so sleek,
> Was the heartiest of them all,
> And would take his place
> With a smiling face
> When refection's bell would call."

For the abbey grounds held bakeries, breweries, fish-ponds, and granaries, and, doubtless, good fat deer were to be had for the hunting, as well as other game, in the adjacent forests.

The position of abbot in these rich monasteries was one not only of dignity, but of power and importance, and the office was sought for by wealthy families for their sons who had entered the church.

Here in Furness, besides being at the head of the monastery, he was chief lord or petty prince of the estate, with certains powers over the liberties of the district.

At the west end of the church are the remains of the great belfry-tower, with massive walls, eleven feet in thickness, supported by buttresses.

Our attention was called to a vast parallelogram, two sides of which were formed by one wall of the church and another of the refectory, in which were the foundations of another great building. Then came the cloisters and the remains of the once beautiful chapter-house, about sixty feet by forty-five, now an open waste of weeds, wild-flowers, and shattered stone-work, and above, indicated by a close range of windows, was the scriptorium. Beneath those windows, in their cool and cosey niches, the monks wrote those beautiful missals which have come down to us, specimens of long and patient labor and of beautiful work in the art of illuminating, exquisite specimens of penmanship, drawing, and coloring, which no typography can equal.

The curious antiquarian will find within the church enclosure, not far from the high altar, various monuments and tombstones that have been collected here from different parts of the ruins. One is of a crusader, cross-legged, with his sword and armor, and others of mailed warriors with shields and helmets, and the sculptured stone coffins of long forgotten abbots.

The guest-hall is a large building distinct by itself, one hundred and thirty feet by fifty, and is forty feet high to the roof. This was also the abbot's lodging, and at one end of it is a private chapel, and at the other a private kitchen, and close by a ruin of mills, ovens, stables, and store-rooms, while huge heaps of shells near the kitchen bear witness that the monks of old had a weakness for oysters. Great windows, including an east window, light the guest-hall, the beautiful roof of which still remains.

Guests of Furness Abbey were royally entertained, if old chronicles are to be believed, and its retainers, tenantry, and other dependents, at the time of its dissolution, sadly missed its aid. But Henry VIII. decided for the suppression of the smaller monasteries, on account, as his bill before Parliament expressed it, of the "manifest synne, carnel, and abominable living daily used and committed," etc. Henry VIII. on abominable living! — Satan reproving sin!

So the old abbey, that seems, from what remains of it, to have been built to have resisted time's assaults for a thousand years, went rapidly to decay after its abandonment in 1537, and three centuries have left but massive walls, ruined arches, pillars, and sculptured fragments, to recall the glories and triumphs of its past history.

Three hundred and seventy-six monasteries, with all their estates and belongings, were by this act confiscated to the king and his heirs, and from that time monastic power and influence in England became a thing of the past.

CHAPTER VII.

How many old English histories and chronicles have been ransacked, how many authorities have been looked up and references investigated, with regard to the history of old Boston in England?

An unpretending, ordinary English town, the chief port of Lincolnshire, and, on looking up its history, found to be what many others in England once were, a Roman town or fortification, it is in the midst of a flat and what was once a barren country, and situated on the river Witham, where it broadens near the sea.

No seaport on the eastern coast of England was more convenient for Holland than old Boston, situated in the rich level fens of Lincolnshire, and reaching the sea by the river Witham. A town of importance in 1204; when a duty was laid on goods, the merchants of London paid £836, and Boston the next largest amount, £780. Boston, also, furnished 17 ships and 361 men for a navy in 1359. But Boston's commercial prosperity began to decline in 1470, on account of the departure of the Hanseatic merchants; and the dissolution of the monasteries within its circuit, soon after, was another loss to it. In the middle of the eighteenth century it had got into a state of commercial decay, but has revived, and is now doing a good business in the corn and cattle trade, giving occupation to a large number of coasting vessels.

It may be said, without perhaps taking too much

credit to ourselves here in New England, that it is the growth and importance of old Boston's modern namesake that caused the former's history to be more carefully looked up in response to the natural curiosity of those of later days to know the early history of the place from whence the name was derived.

The original name of Boston, it is supposed, was derived from St. Botolph, a pious Saxon, who lived about the middle of the seventh century, and who founded a monastery there, which was destroyed by an army of marauding Danes. In 1541 an author (Leland) wrote of it as "Botolphstowne," with its "three colleges of Friars — Gray, Black, and Augustine," and in 1565 its population was about 2380 persons, according to a MS. in the British Museum. In 1791 it is noted as a flourishing town on both sides of the river Witham, and protected from overflow by artificial banks. But old Boston was not so progressive as its modern namesake, for the returns of its population from 1768 to 1831 showed an increase from 3500 to about 11,250 population. But old Boston probably sent more than any other town in England of its best and worthiest citizens to colonize America.

Old Boston is where the spirit of Puritanism was kept alive and flourishing, chiefly through the agency of John Cotton, during the period of whose ministry Winthrop and his company took their departure for the New World. Cotton himself followed a short time afterwards. Interesting to modern Bostonians, therefore, is this ancient town of Lincolnshire, thus associated with the Pilgrim Fathers, who laid the foundations of this country, the mightiest of republics.

The Lincolnshire fens are now so well drained and cultivated that they are no longer the barren morasses and desert lands described in the old chronicles, but simply a long, level stretch of green meadow-land that we traverse as we approach old Boston, and the first indication of it that we get is the tall tower rising far into the air, a notable landmark, which was of service, in ancient times, to mariners in determining their course.

But there is nothing that savors of antiquity in the large, well appointed railway station, and, leaving the train, we take an omnibus for the Peacock and Royal Inn, situated upon the public square or market-place. We at once established our respectability and importance by ordering two rooms and a private parlor. It was the same class of country inn so familiar to travellers, with its commercial room, tap-room, bar and barmaid, curious and bewildering passages, low-ceiled rooms and old furniture.

But we must look around the old town, which is now the centre of a rich, agricultural district. Its chief glory is its cathedral, which the American pilgrim of to-day visits with peculiar interest, as the one where his pious forefathers worshipped.

St. Botolph's Church in old Boston, where for twenty years John Cotton promulgated his religious teachings, was indeed in striking contrast with the humble building in which he afterwards officiated in our new Boston, for this grand, gray, and lofty-towered cathedral will take in thousands of worshippers within its walls. Cotton left England in 1633 (a graduate of Trinity College) for America. The settlement of the modern Boston was so small at that period that but one small meeting-house was required for the whole community down to 1648, and that until 1640 had mud walls and a thatched roof. This primitive building in new Boston, history tells us, was situated on what is now the south side of State Street, but was succeeded in 1640 by a more commodious wooden building on Washington Street, nearly opposite State Street, where it stood for seventy years, until destroyed by fire.

But let us turn our attention to the grand church of old Boston. The foundation of this church is very ancient. History says the church was given to the great Benedictine abbey of St. Mary, in York, by Alan Rufus of Brittany, in the reign of William the Conqueror. The abbot and convent made an exchange of it with the crown in the reign of Edward the Fourth (about 1475), and the Knights of St. John of Jerusalem exchanged some of their lands in Leicestershire for it, soon after, and held it until the dissolution of religious houses in England.

The magnificent tower of this church, the loftiest in the kingdom, is said to have been laid on wool-sacks, from the fact that, at the period when it was built, Boston was one of the ten shipping ports of England, and the principal one as to the extent of its shipments, doing a large business in wool, leather, and hides, especially the first named commodity, and, curiously enough, Boston in New England is the principal wool-market of the United States to-day. Lincolnshire is also to-day one of the principal wool-growing districts of England.

The tower of the church is said to have been built after the model of the great church of Antwerp, and is 262 feet 9 inches in height. It is very graceful, with great Gothic windows on each of the three sides in the lower story to the height of the roof of the nave. This story contains what is known as the great west window, as well as the west door. Above, in the second division of the steeple, are two Gothic pointed windows on each of the three sides. Above this, in a third division, is one window on each side again. This is the bell-chamber, and at the base of this division an external gallery runs around the tower; and above this is a great lantern, formed by arches bent diagonally over the angles of the tower, making an octagon of the upper part.

This lantern served as a beacon, and was lighted at night, and "rose like a Pharos above the surrounding levels."

The external surface of this superb tower is covered with panel-work, and the first story has effective shafted buttresses and statues. The great western door has some beautiful carved work, and the lantern, with its two-light window in each face of the octagon, is a light and graceful crown to the whole structure.

A history of Lincolnshire churches says that, from the changes of architecture which are visible in the building, it took two hundred years in erecting, and was carried forward during the reigns of the different sovereigns. Entering by the Gothic archway of the south porch and through the curious and elaborately carved ancient doors, we find ourselves directly in front of an elegantly carved font, capacious in size, presenting a perfect wealth of carved work, the upper part or brim being encircled by a wreath of vine-leaves exquisitely wrought from the stone. This font was made from a solid block of what is called Ancaster stone, a white, clear, grained material, and was presented to the church by A. J. Beresford Hope, in 1853.

Once inside, you may look far up to the grand stone vaulting of the tower, which is 156 feet above the floor. There, in different sections of the beautiful groined ceiling, with its rings or octagons of carved work beautifully executed, in the centre of each, are sculptured bosses bearing appropriate religious designs, such as Agnus Dei, angels, and emblems. A few steps forward and the eye may take in the interior. The nave, with its seven pointed arches on each side, on their clustered pillars, the magnificent west window, and the panelled surface of the lofty walls form a grand and imposing view.

The lofty roof appears to be of carved oak, and the whole of the nave is filled with oaken seats facing the east. The pulpit, which is against one of the pillars on the south side of the nave, is a fine piece of carved work in oak, hexagonal in shape, and its decorations the handiwork of artificers in Queen Elizabeth's time.

The only ancient monuments we saw in the church were in one of the aisles; one of an unknown knight, a full-length figure in full armor, helm on head, and sword at his hip, and feet resting on a lion. The figure was recumbent on a tomb, with representations of crowned angels bearing shields, the whole cut from alabaster. Another monument was that of a reclining lady, upon an altar of black marble.

In the beautiful chancel are the ancient stalls, over seventy in number, many of which have been restored and their small turn-up seats decorated, as was usual by the ancient wood-carvers, with grotesque caricatures, saints and burlesque scenes, as if trying to divert the mind of the probable occupant from his devotions or serious thoughts. Uncomfortable as these ancient seats were, they were contrived so that, should the occupant slumber and lose the pose required to keep the seat upright, he would be tumbled upon the pavement, so that really he performed penance with his devotion.

The carved oak communion-table of St. Botolph's, and

the two tall candelabra, twelve feet high, bearing seven lights each, will attract the visitor's attention, and the magnificent east window command his admiration.

This window contains seven great upright divisions or sections, above which is the pointed Gothic arch, of stone tracery. The lower sections are filled with what is called the "Genealogy of our Lord," portrayed in the beautiful colored glass. There are large-sized figures representing the Virgin and Child, the Magi bringing offerings, the four Evangelists, the Crucifixion, Jesus Sitting in Judgment, and other figures, to the number of twenty-one, all beautifully executed and surrounded by a wealth of ornamentation. Above, in the openings of the stone tracery of the arch, are representations of the archangels Michael, Gabriel, and Raphael, surrounded by numerous beautiful designs and decorations.

Americans, especially New Englanders, will, of course, be interested in and visit the South-west Chapel, which is known as the Cotton Chapel. This was restored in 1855, mainly through the efforts of our distinguished fellow-citizen Edward Everett, who raised a subscription in this country, and was aided by George Peabody, Russell Sturgis, and Joshua Bates, then American bankers in London.

An amount was realized sufficient to cleanse, repair, and thoroughly restore the entire chapel, as well as to place a beautiful window, filled with stained glass, at the west end of it, and a memorial tablet upon the wall.

The following is a translation of the Latin inscription, composed by Mr. Everett, which is upon the tablet: —

"In perpetual remembrance of John Cotton, who, during the reign of James and Charles, was for many years a grave, skilful, learned, and laborious Vicar of this Church. Afterwards, on account of the lamentable troubles in religious matters in his own country, he sought a new settlement in a new world, and remained, even to the end of his life, a pastor and teacher of the greatest reputation and of the greatest authority in the first church of Boston, in New England, which received its venerable name in honor of Cotton: ccxxv. years having passed away since his migration, his descendants and the American citizens of Boston were invited to this pious work by their English brethren, in order that the name of an illustrious man, the love and honor of both worlds, might not longer be banished from that noble temple in which he diligently, learnedly, and sacredly expounded the divine oracles for so many years; and they have willingly and gratefully caused this shrine to be restored, and this tablet to be erected, in the year of our recovered salvation 1855."

I venture to give also a list of the subscribers to the fund, as being names of typical Bostonians of the New England city, and standing for men who have been foremost in adding to and upholding those attributes which make modern Boston honored among its peers: —

"Charles Francis Adams, William Turrell Andrews, Nathan Appleton, William Appleton, George Bancroft, Martin Brimmer, Edward Brooks, Gorham Brooks, Sidney Brooks, Peter Chardon Brooks, John P. Cushing, Edward Everett, Nathaniel Langdon Frothingham, John Chipman Gray, Abbott Lawrence, John Amory Lowell, Jonathan Phillips, William Hickling Prescott, David Sears, Nathaniel Bradstreet Shurtleff, Jared Sparks, John Eliot Thayer, Frederic Tudor, John Collins Warren."

The dimensions of St. Botolph are given as 245 feet long and 98 feet wide within the walls, and we were told that there were 365 steps to the top of the tower, equalling the number of days in the year; twelve columns supporting the main roof, the number of months in the year; fifty-two windows, equalling the weeks; seven doors, the days in the week; twenty-four steps to the south porch library, hours of the day; and sixty steps to the chancel roof, minutes in the hour. The church is said to be the finest parish church in the kingdom, and it certainly impresses one by its perfect harmony of proportions, of clustered pillars, massive arches, groined roof, and lofty tower.

Old Boston town is like many other English towns that one visits, and has little of interest to the tourist except the church. The houses of the older part of the town are not over two or three stories high, and built of dark-red bricks. It can rival modern Boston as it once was in some of its narrow streets and quaint old alley-ways.

The inhabitants of old Boston do not appear to have appreciated the commercial value of antiquities, and the traveller who looks for memorials of the Pilgrims and John Cotton will be doomed to disappointment. The old vicarage in which Cotton lived was taken down in 1850. The only two antique buildings of any particular significance are the old town-hall and Shodfriars' Hall, both near the market-place.

The former is an old, blackened brick edifice, with a Gothic door and big Gothic window over it, and it is here that Brewster and others of the Pilgrims were said to have been brought up for examination before the magistrates, and in the lower story of the building are said to have been imprisoned, in some dark little dens that are shown there.

In the basement story is an ancient kitchen, of considerable size, where cooking used to be done for civic feasting in the great hall above, in the second story, where two or three hundred guests could be accommodated. This building is really all, except the church already described, that can in any way be connected with the Pilgrims.

Shodfriars' Hall is a quaint old building, of wood and plaster, that has been braced up and restored. Old Boston is to-day busy improving some of its advantages, that have long been neglected, for down at the river-front we find the work of building a new dock for shipping had been performed in excellent, solid, substantial style. Boston owed its early commercial importance to its geographical position and its river and harbor, while for a port of transit to the north of France, Holland, and Flanders it was one of the best on the east coast of England. In their modern improvements for shipping and receiving merchandise, the people of the place wisely conclude to make the most of the position, which still has many commercial advantages for receiving goods from the interior for export and merchandise from abroad for distribution. A large area is enclosed, on the river front, and storehouses have been built for merchandise, and tracks been laid connecting with different railways of the kingdom, so that the wool, corn, and cattle business may be fostered, pushed, and improved by old Boston's merchants of to-day.

CHAPTER VIII.

BERLIN.

IT is a long leap from old Boston to Berlin, but the reader is spared the details of the journey, including the discomforts of the British Channel, which have, after so many years, only been partially alleviated. Since my last visit to the Prussian capital, some dozen years ago, there has been a notable improvement in the hotels of that city. A fine new one, the Continental, at the time of my visit (1886), was admirably kept, and with most of those appurtenances and appointments that Americans know so well how to appreciate, such as a good elevator, luxurious bath-rooms, and a fairly good *cuisine* — except the iron-clad bread that prevails here. The outer crusts of the breakfast-rolls require a blacksmith's hammer, or the teeth of a crocodile, to crack them. Berlin is a good point from which to start for St. Petersburg, I was told, and so I found it to be, as the sequel will prove.

The American flag, hanging out from a window on the Unter den Linden, had a most homelike and friendly look to it, and the hospitable quarters of the American Exchange in Europe, which it indicated, are pleasant indeed to the wandering American tourist, for here he can hear his own language spoken, read Boston and New York newspapers, and hear the latest news from home by telegraph, including embezzlements, forgeries, flights to Canada, railroad accidents, and terrible conflagrations; all these events, having precedence as news to be sent over the ocean, make America appear a perfect pandemonium of crime and horror when it is seen at this distance.

Large, enterprising, and well governed as Berlin is, the American cannot fail to notice how much more quiet, methodical, and deliberate everything is there than in any of our American cities. The tremendous rush, hurry, and spirit of briskness and enterprise are lacking, although, since I was last there, horse-cars traverse the streets, conductors signal you and shout out the streets and localities as they pass, and the gilded youth dash rapidly through the broad avenues in their carriages, and crowds throng the great retail business streets; but there is not that restlessness or nervousness that characterizes an American city, and to the average American tourist there is a feeling of restful comfort. I certainly felt some degree of it in noticing that three or four days were required to make a new turn-out and to relay about one hundred feet of horse-railroad track in one of the streets, which would have been accomplished in one-fourth of the time in New York or Boston, and, it is but justice to add, been about one-fourth as well done in the matter of thoroughness of workmanship and the good condition in which street and pavement were left.

"But I am going to Russia in a day or two," I remarked to a friend whom I met one day on Unter den Linden. "What step shall I take first?"

"Secure James Pilley, the English guide there, if you can; he has lived over twenty years in St. Petersburg, speaks Russian like a native, knows every sight and everything worth seeing in the country."

Prompt use of the telegraph, and of letters from a

friend of the noted guide, in Berlin, achieved the desired result.

Now, then, as to the method and manner of going from Berlin to St. Petersburg. First, it is absolutely necessary to have a passport, and this must first be viséd by the American and then by the Russian consul. Then you must get some money changed into Russian paper currency for immediate use, if required on the road or on arrival. Of course, in Russian cities like St. Petersburg, Moscow, Odessa, etc., your letter of credit is as promptly recognized as elsewhere.

The journey by rail from Berlin to St. Petersburg, which you begin at 8:30 in the morning, occupies all that day and all night, and all the next day until 10 P. M.

First to obtain through tickets, which are bought at a railroad ticket office on the Unter den Linden, and in which transaction we called in the aid of one of the English-speaking clerks of the American Exchange.

The price of a ticket from Berlin to the Russian frontier was 67 marks and a fraction in the first-class carriages, or about $17 United States currency; from the frontier to St. Petersburg you pay, in Russian roubles, an additional 36 roubles, the value of a rouble being about fifty cents, which makes $18 additional, or $35 for the whole distance. The proper thing to do is to buy a through ticket two days in advance, at the office above mentioned, and also to have the ticket clerk telegraph on to the frontier and get answer to your despatch, securing a sleeping-compartment for you in the train that will leave there soon after your arrival and custom-house examination.

As an old traveller I took this precaution, and likewise to get answer back that the compartment was secured. I then had the name of the official at the Russian frontier station, to whom this despatch had been sent, written down for me, both in Russian and German, by the clerk in attendance at the Berlin office, with a line from him in the former language to the clerk at the frontier.

The effort to procure a modern guide-book was fruitless. Murray's latest was twelve years old (1875), Badaeker has issued none, and Harper's was unattainable. As to luggage, each passenger is allowed fifty-six pounds free, and no charge was made for the hand-luggage; for some unaccountable reason, however, it cost more to bring the same amount of luggage out of Russia than it did to carry it into that empire. I could not get much information respecting meals *en route*, or where they were to be taken; in fact, very little of the real practical information one really wants; but, having had experience at German and Prussian railroad restaurants, where beer, sausage, raw-ham sandwiches, and tobacco are the chief creature-comforts provided for hungry mortals, we took the precaution to have a cold fowl, some of the sweet, iron-crusted bread, and a bottle of claret put up, to provide against accidents; and it was well we did, for as long as we were in Prussian territory, it was one unceasing deluge of beer, while the sausage, raw-ham sandwiches, cheese, and similar comestibles were anything but inviting. But, presto! after entering Russian territory, the style changed to the well appointed French restaurant, with light, soft bread, coffee, clean, un-beer-stained buffets with French cakes, light wines, appetizing goodies, and fruits.

The first-class railway carriage in which we started from Berlin was built somewhat after the style of what is known in America as the Mann Boudoir Car. Our compartment had seats for six persons, and the approach to it was by an aisle running along the side of the car, which was furnished with lavatories at each end. Our compartment was abundantly furnished with racks and hooks for small baggage, which are so much needed and so seldom provided in the Pullman and Wagner cars of America. The seats were arranged as in the English cars — three back to the locomotive and three facing it. There were five of us occupying the compartment — two German or Prussian merchants, a Russian young gentleman, myself and companion.

It is the rule posted up that, if none of those in the carriage object, any one may smoke; and two of our companions were puffing like furnaces, to my own infinite disgust at least. Indeed, upon the continent the infliction of tobacco smoke that a non-smoker has to endure will rival any of the same nuisance, coupled even though it is with expectoration, in America. It does seem as if some travellers cannot enjoy a mountain ascent, a railway ride, a sight-seeing stroll, or a diligence journey, without sucking at cigarettes or pipes, and blowing this offensive cloud into the faces of their fellow-travellers.

I remember that the open carriages of the railway up Mt. Rigi, in Switzerland, were an excuse for the half-dozen Frenchmen and Germans to puff their vile cigarettes and abominable pipes, sending back their vile odors into the nostrils of those seated behind them, and seriously interfering with one of the grandest panoramic views ever seen. And the notices respecting smoking in all the railroad carriages of the continent, the carriages provided especially for smokers there as well as at home, prove what tyranny is exercised by the tobacco-smoker over the rest of the community. One satisfaction to the man who does not smoke is having a lady as his travelling companion abroad; she saves him this infliction of smoke in railway carriages, diligences, and elsewhere; whereas, if alone, being a man, it is presumed he has no right to object.

One of our smoking companions left after a four-hour ride, and another when we reached Kreuze, and the other two at Königsberg, the ancient Prussian capital. The remaining passenger, a little, light-haired Russian whose acquaintance we made over a glass of claret, proved to be the private secretary of the Duchess of Edinburgh. on his way to St. Petersburg. He spoke English fluently, and was of much service to us.

The railroad route which we took from Berlin was *via* Kreuze, Königsberg, Eydkuhnen, Wierzbolow, Wilna, Dunaburg, Pskov, Luga, and other towns with unpronounceable names. Eydkuhnen and Wierzbolow are respectively the Prussian and Russian frontier stations, and are about one mile apart. Luggage is examined at the latter as you go into Russia, and at the former as you come out. The distance from Berlin to the Russian frontier is 450 miles, and from thence to Petersburg 560, a total of 1010 miles. It might be accomplished in much less time than is taken, were it not for the comparatively low rate of speed, and the Russian custom of stopping twenty minutes or half an hour at every large station.

They have a custom on the railroad line of ringing a bell just outside the station, as a warning for passengers, which is peculiar and effective where stops of any length of time are made, which is this: Five minutes before the train is to start, an official runs the tongue of the bell sharply around its rim, and concludes with one sharp tap ; two minutes later the tongue is again scraped around it, concluding with two smart taps ; and two minutes later still, it is scraped around three times, concluding with three smart taps, the last signal, and that for closing the car doors ; for one minute after this last bell-tap, the conductor or guard sounds his sharp whistle that all is right, the engineer responds with a like blast, and the train starts.

This system prevailed all along this line in Prussia and Russia, and was a good one, being easily understood by all, the first alarm giving time to pay for one's meal and start, and the second letting you know that two minutes remained to return to your carriage.

At midnight we arrived at the Russian frontier, and, on descending upon the brilliantly lighted platform of the station, the first person we encountered was a tall soldier, in gray overcoat, dog-skin and scarlet shako, surmounted by a pompon. He was also booted and spurred, and wore a long sabre. as if just dismounted from a cavalry troop. He pointed to an open door, and ejaculated :

" Passe-ports."

We delivered our passports, and, on entering, found ourselves in one of those large rooms with a raised platform running round its entire length for the baggage examination, so familiar to European travellers who have crossed frontiers on the continent.

The luggage was rapidly brought in, and the production of a few copecks (a five-copeck piece is the size of an old-fashioned United States cent) caused the porters to place your trunks as you want them. It is well to remember that Russia is pre-eminently a country of bribes, and that the quiet passage of a few copecks to laborers, or of roubles to higher officials, accomplishes wonders in the way of convenience, especially for American travellers, who seem to be, when known as such, regarded with more favor than those of other nationalities.

The passports were all carried to one end of the room, to the desk of a uniformed official, and from thence were brought forward, two or three at a time, by his subordinates, and held up for the owners to claim, who afterwards pointed out their luggage for examination. Observing that this examination was more thorough with some trunks than others, my companion proceeded to the official desk, and, after profoundly salaaming with marked respect the great man at that post, proceeded in the German tongue to acquaint him that two American tourists had honored him with their company, and would he deign to detail two of his officers to examine and affix his *visé* to their luggage, etc? Moreover, would he accept the assurances of our distinguished consideration?

The effect of this profound deference by two first-class passengers to this great chief, before a circle of third-class passengers, as well as his subordinates, surrounding him, had its effect. Our passports were promptly handed over with a deferential bow, two officials were detailed, who proceeded at once to our luggage, which went through the slightest form possible of inspection, and we were handed cards which passed us by the guard at the door into the buffet and waiting-room.

At this place we were to obtain our tickets and places in the sleeping-car for St. Petersburg, which had been telegraphed for from Berlin; and here the foresight of having the official's name in Russian, and the line from the Berlin clerk, came in play, for, although the old fellow spoke and understood German, he at first stoutly denied the receipt of any dispatch, until that paper was shown him, when he promptly produced two tickets for what proved an excellent sleeping-compartment.

We were detained for over an hour at the frontier, and it was nearly 2 A. M. before our couches were made ready by the car porter. The car was divided into a series of two and four-berthed compartments, opening upon an aisle running the whole length of the railway carriage, with lavatories at each end. The running was remarkably easy and comfortable, and we enjoyed a good night's rest, breakfasting in the morning, at eight, at a good, clean, well kept buffet, upon chops, eggs, hot rolls, and deliciously flavored tea, served, Russian fashion, with thin slices of lemon floating on its surface. Chocolate, cold meats, fowls, good sandwiches, and all the eatables usually found at French restaurants were provided at these buffets, which, as a general thing, I am constrained to say, were far superior to those on the lines of many of our great lines of railroads in America.

We found our Russian railway carriage to be comfortable and well ventilated, and one peculiarity of the water-faucets was that they send a stream upwards so as to fall upon the hands, and no stopper was in the basins to retain the water. While at the stations where we stopped, the women who were in waiting with water for those passengers who desired to perform their ablutions poured the water upon their hands, in the Eastern style and according to Russian custom.

The scenery through which we passed was of but little interest, the surface of the country reminding one of some of the wilder parts of the State of Maine, while the stations gave us but little opportunity to see anything of the towns except a distant view of them. The houses of the common people appear to be rough log shanties, and the fields rudely and poorly cultivated.

The uninteresting character of the landscape, as seen from the windows of the railway carriage, made the English novels, which all old travellers take care to provide themselves with, welcome companions; but we were heartily glad when, at half-past ten that night, the train rolled into the well lighted railway station at St. Petersburg, and, as we emerged from the railway carriage we were greeted by a well dressed Englishman, calling us by name in our own language, and stating that a carriage was in waiting for us.

This was James Pilley, the English guide, a compact, well built man, about forty-five years of age, who gave a few rapid orders to some men in attendance respecting the conveyance of our luggage, and then escorted us, through the crowd of drosky-drivers that surrounded the station, to a well appointed two-horse carriage, into which we stepped with him, and were soon speeding along through the broad streets to the hotel, some two miles away. On through the well lighted streets we rode, until at last the Grand Hôtel d'Europe was reached, a building nearly as large, and with a much more extensive frontage, than the Fifth Avenue Hotel, New York.

The entrance hall of the hotel was far better arranged and more comfortable than the Grand or Metropole in London, and the room accommodations were better and cheaper.

Here, on arrival, we were received, at the foot of the marble steps that led up to the main floor, by a head-waiter, who spoke English and French. Inside, at the right, was a large office, where the chief porter, also a linguist, ran the business of the hotel, such as receiving letters, caring for room-keys, and in all respects like the American hotel clerk except that there was no counter separating his domain from public intrusion. At the left was a large, convenient, and well lighted reading-room, with newspapers and magazines, including American and English newspapers, but I noticed portions of the latter had been blacked out, or completely erased with black ink, by the post-office authorities, before being permitted to be displayed.

A whole page of the London *Punch* had been thus treated, which, I afterwards ascertained, contained a caricature of the Russian Bear and Bulgaria; and a half-column of the London *Times*, reflecting upon Russia's policy, had been similarly obliterated.

This is performed by the censor of the press, through whose hands all publications that come into the empire pass before being delivered to the parties to whom they are directed.

He has a large office, which, in general appearance, resembles the editorial rooms of a great American daily newspaper. A large corps of assistants open the mails, and submit to him all questionable matter. Anything reflecting upon the government or its policy, or the royal family, is promptly tabooed, and a roller of black ink is passed over it, in newspaper or magazine, leaving a dense black space, through which not a single word can be discerned.

Newspapers in Russia, even those favoring and flattering the government, do not amount to much. The censorship of every article referring to the subjects above named, or even to visits of the royal family or facts relating to the army, causes so much delay in the delivery of the paper that it is hardly worth while to attempt the publication of news relating to politics, or to any one or anything connected with the empire. Then, Russia is far from being a newspaper-reading nation. Right here in St. Petersburg it was amazing how few of the common work-people and artisans could read and write. Not one in a dozen of the drosky-drivers could read the signboards in the streets, and I do not recall a single instance of seeing one of them, or any of the artizan or laboring class, reading a newspaper or printed sheet.

The Russian alphabet is different from that used in the rest of Europe, and is composed of thirty-six characters, which seem to have been adapted from the Greek alphabet, with the addition of a certain number of new characters. These characters are Greek, however, to the common people, and for their information the front and sides of most of the stores are adorned with pictorial representations of what may be had within.

The butcher has legs of mutton, joints, or an ox delineated on his sign; the baker, heaps of bread; the music-dealer, horns, fiddles, and drums; the clothing-dealer, portraits of coats, stockings, and other garments; — and this illustrative sign-painting is carried to such an extent that some of it had to be translated to us by our guide — such as, for instance, that of a midwife, and another of a surgeon, or some practitioner who drew teeth and applied leeches.

It is stated that the proportion of ignorant to educated people in the empire is nearly seventy per cent., and that of the one hundred million inhabitants of Russia sixty million were either among the serfs freed by Alexander II., twenty-five years ago, or their children.

CHAPTER IX.

THE Grand Hôtel d'Europe is situated upon the corner of Place Michael and Nevski Prospect, the latter a very wide and straight street three miles long, with a modern horse-railway running through the middle of it. This grand thoroughfare is the great Broadway of the city, and has several superb churches, the Alexander Theatre, Imperial Library, and other notable buildings upon it. We were escorted to our room, a large double-bedded apartment in the third story, the four windows commanding an extensive view of the broad avenue as far as the eye could reach. This apartment was handsomely furnished, like the leading hotels of America, with mirrors, sofas, arm-chairs, French clocks, and with the addition of screens to place before the beds, which were excellent, and writing-tables for the guests. The waiters who answered our bell spoke German, and we got on very well with them. The price per day for this room was three dollars for two persons, with an additional charge of twenty-five cents a day for service. A good table d'hôte dinner was served for a rouble and a half, about seventy-five cents; indeed, I was surprised at the excellence of the cuisine, the promptness of the service, and the moderate rate of charge, as I had been led to expect the opposite from all English accounts I had read, George Augustus Sala's included.

As soon as we were fairly domiciled in our apartment, we were waited upon by the English-speaking head-waiter with the hotel book, in which we inscribed our names, and then surrendered to him our passports, for which the landlord of the hotel became responsible, as he must report us and take them to the chief of police.

Indeed, the landlord thus becomes the custodian of, and in a measure responsible for, his foreign guests, inasmuch as they cannot leave St. Petersburg without these important documents, or, if required while there, can be held till they are produced ; it will be seen also there is not much danger of the hotel guest's departing without satisfying his host as to his intention and where he is going, as he must notify him the day previous, in order that the passport may be obtained properly *viséd* for that purpose.

On rising after a good night's rest, we looked out upon the broad avenue from our windows upon the novel sights before us ; nearly opposite was a little one-story, open-fronted temple, erected to some saint or for some holy deed, and within was a shrine with burning candles, a holy-water font, and the usual decorations. Every Russian who passed this on foot raised his hat and crossed himself; some of the more devout halted, crossed their arms upon their breasts, bowed three times, and repeated a prayer. Others, besides dipping the fingers in the font, took a drink therefrom in a tiny tin cup prepared for that purpose.

The healthfulness or cleanliness of drinking water in which hundreds of hands have been dipped, including the begrimed ones of workmen and those of filthy beggars, may well be questioned. Indeed, it is affirmed that infectious diseases have been transmitted in this manner. The more superstitious Russian, however, may imagine that by drinking the water he carries away more holiness than can be conveyed to the forehead by a touch of the finger.

It was a novel sight to see a modern street-car pass with the roof crowded with passengers, every one of whom took off his hat and made the sign of the cross as they went by this shrine. Those who passed without reverence, we were told, were Tartars. They are largely employed as laborers and servants in St. Petersburg, and may be distinguished from having neither beards nor moustaches, all hair being carefully plucked from their faces.

The curiously lettered signs, the bulb-topped steeples, reminding one of Turkish or Moorish architecture, and in some cases having the cross rising from out the crescent on their steeples, the tall fire or watch towers, the curiously costumed drosky-drivers, and the occasionally sheepskin-clad peasant, all were novelties.

The costume of the working-people seems to be invariably a pair of long boots, into which the coarse trousers are thrust, after the style of a California miner. Then the Russian wears his red or blue flannel shirt outside his pantaloons, and over it a coarse, brown, dirty, crash-towel-looking blouse. A face of dense stupidity, surrounded by a forest of unkempt hair and beard, completes his description.

Acting upon the suggestion of our guide, we engaged a first-class two-horse open carriage by the day. In fact, having but comparatively brief time for our sight-seeing, we gave our guide *carte blanche* to do the best possible, in order that we might make the best use of the time at our command.

The ordinary droskies are common and dirty enough, but good ones can be had by those who want them. The drosky is a low, four-wheeled carriage drawn by one horse and with seats for two passengers. The driver sits upon a seat slightly elevated, in front, and the space for the passenger is barely sufficient to accommodate his drawn-up knees.

The drosky is to St. Petersburg what the cab is to London and is found at all railway stations and on the principal streets. Many of the drivers are young countrymen who have been attracted to the city by the large wages paid to drosky-drivers, about a dollar a day. The more fashionable carriages are of the same model as our victorias, well fitted, with good springs, and as comfortable as could be desired.

It is said the Russian drosky-driver has no regular charge, and, like his prototype all over the world, considers those who use his vehicle his regular prey. How tourists with no knowledge of the Russian tongue get on with him, I am at loss to know. Our excellent guide spared us all difficulties of this description, however.

A drosky engaged by the day means from about 8 A. M. till midnight, and the price of our carriage, which was a sort of open barouche, better than ordinary droskies, was ten roubles a day, with an extra rouble and a half for the driver.

Our guide sat upon the box with the driver, and we occupied the back seat of the vehicle, which was drawn by two splendid black stallions. The harness, with the exception of traces, was exceedingly light, and we sped through the streets at the rate of six or eight miles an hour, at a smart trot, the peculiar cry of our driver warning all humbler vehicles, and wandering pedestrians, to get out of the way, which they did most promptly and speedily.

Our ride was made all the more enjoyable from the

fact that the wheels of the vehicle were tired with india-rubber, so that we were spared the rattle of the wheels as an interruption to conversation or our guide's descriptions. The driver — or *isvostchik*, as he is called in Russian — has an odd costume. His hat looks like an old-fashioned bell-crowned beaver, that had been razed by taking out the middle portion; a long, green sort of dressing-gown, reaching nearly to the heels, was buttoned over to the left, and ornamented with bunches of silver buttons at the right side, and bound round with a bright-colored sash; the long boots, into which the baggy pantaloons were thrust, completed the costume. The Russian driver seldom whips his horses; ours merely held a short-handled whip out at right angles with his body, and his horses were off at full speed. He was a capital driver, and whirled us through the streets by aid of voice, rein, and whip signal with great skill.

What strikes one, at first, in St. Petersburg, is the grand scale on which everything is laid out; the long streets, twice as wide as Broadway, or like the great avenues at Washington, enormous squares in which thousands of troops might be manœuvred, huge public buildings and churches, great barracks with thousands of feet of frontage, — everything appears to have been projected as for some stupendous capital and huge population yet to be.

The population of St. Petersburg is said to be over seven hundred thousand; its great, broad, and regular streets and huge squares cover more than thirty square miles of territory. And when you come to reflect that this vast and magnificent city is built upon a quaking morass, and its huge churches and palaces, that overwhelm you with their vastness and splendor, are built upon a forest of piles, sunk in a trembling bog, but a little above the level of the Baltic Sea, and that snow and ice reign here for five months of the year, you are astonished at the pertinacity of Peter in choosing a spot with so many natural difficulties to overcome, and still more astonished at the manner in which those obstacles were met and defeated, and at the extent and splendor of a city that two centuries ago was not in existence.

The first brick building here was built in 1710, and the great structure known as the Admiralty started in 1711. The difficulties of building the city must have been tremendous. But, tremendous as they were, that gigantic, irrepressible, savage genius, Peter the Great, overcame them, but at a terrific expense of human life. The conscripted peasants from every part of Russia, that like the ancient Israelites wrought under the taskmaster's lash, must have perished by thousands in the effort. But the effort was successful, and stands a wonder to the generation that to-day contemplates the result.

The river Neva runs into the Bay of Cronstadt, breaking up as it does so into little branches, and forming numerous islands near the mouth. St. Petersburg rests on the bank of the river, and these islands are connected with the latter by the superb Nicholas Bridge, a structure with grand iron arches, and piers of granite of great strength, built, evidently, to resist the fall floods and spring outgo of ice. There are other bridges, floating ones, so constructed as to be removed during the winter. The Nicholas Bridge, however, is a broad and beautiful highway, as well as a splendid specimen of bridge-building.

The tall fire-towers, with their watchmen, are a feature here. These lofty towers communicate with each other at night by means of a series of colored lanterns, and by day by other signals, indicating in exactly what quarter a fire breaks out, and where assistance is wanted. Fires are dreaded here, especially during the winter, when the river is frozen over; these towers and the spires, huge churches, the enormous and splendidly built government buildings, the massive granite quays, bridges and canals, with their crowd of boats and shipping, strike the stranger with astonishment. The streets are all broad and well kept, narrow lanes and alleys being the exception.

There are soldiers in groups, singly, and in pairs, seen at every turn, in their long and not over-clean coats and flat caps, the Cossacks of the Guard appearing to be the cleanest, best kept, and most soldier-like.

There were said to be eighty thousand troops in the garrison; one does not need to be long in Russia to be impressed with her great military strength and resources. A recent article published in England by Sir Charles Dilke, extracts from which were published in the Russian papers, states that Russia is the gainer from the awe she inspires on all hands as a power of unknown strength. She has not only a large army on paper, but also in fact. In times of peace, the army of Russia — including the "irregulars" and the Cossacks — numbers eight hundred and ninety thousand men, while in war she can and would raise an army of four million, and, in case of need, six million men. The Russians have as many field-pieces (cannon) as the French or the German, while the Russian cavalry is equal in numbers and efficiency to the cavalry of both these western powers combined, and would outnumber the combined cavalry of Germany and Austria. Sir Charles, besides, fails to see anything desperate in the financial difficulties of Russia, considering that, with her practically limitless natural resources, — Siberia alone equalling the United States in extent of territory, — the country seems bound to yield large revenues.

The official report on the Russian army lately published contains the following particulars: On the 1st of January, 1886, there were 824,762 men, including 8000 volunteers, in the active army.

The reserve amounted to 1,600,815, in addition, thus making a total of 2,425,557 soldiers whom Russia could bring into the field at need. In Germany the maximum of the regular army and the *landwehr* combined is computed at 1,800,000 men. Moreover, Russia has at its disposal 2,160,000 militia, liable to be called upon in time of war to recruit the ranks of the regular army.

The number of young men annually liable to the conscription is 852,000, of whom about one-half are exempted by lot. If the term of service were reduced from five to three years, the state would, in a short time, be able to have 4,000,000 regular troops, without having recourse to the militia reserves. The Russian journals refer with jubilation to these practically inexhaustible resources as compared with other countries.

At present there is no such thing as a force of irregulars, but it is pointed out that nuclei for troops of that description exist in ample measure among the tribes of Central Asia, of the Caucasus, and of the Transcaspian provinces.

In addition to 235.000 conscripts to be called out this year, 2400 new recruits are to be raised in Kuban, Terek, and the Transcaucasian province.

Our first day's sight-seeing took us to St. Isaac's

Cathedral, which is at one end of the Nevski Prospect, the monastery of Alexander Nevski, three miles away, being at the other.

St. Isaac's stands in one of the largest open spaces in the city, and is surrounded by other magnificent buildings and monuments; on approaching it we passed through a grand and lofty archway, from each side of which, in a sort of semicircle, extended wings of tall and handsome buildings, forming one side of a vast square, in the centre of which stood the Alexander Column, surmounted by the figure of an angel bearing a cross. It is a monolith of red granite, eighty-four feet in height, and stands on a pedestal twenty-four feet high, the whole height being one hundred and fifty feet. The shaft is the largest monolith in the world. The pedestal is a beautifully finished piece of work, and weighs four hundred tons. It is an enormous cube of twenty-five feet, of red granite, and bears the inscription: "To Alexander I., Grateful Russia."

Opposite stands the Winter Palace, which, with the exception of the palace of Versailles and the Vatican at Rome, is the largest palace in the world designed for a residence, and at the left rises the magnificent cathedral, grand in its proportions and simple in its architecture. One should stand and view it for a while, to take in all its noble porticos, magnificent dome, grand entrances, superb, highly polished monoliths, and its wealth of carved stone-work. It is the grandest cathedral in Northern Europe, and I cannot recall one, save St. Peter's at Rome, that so impressed me with its grandeur and beauty.

It is built in the usual form of a Greek cross, of four equal sides, having an imposing entrance at each of these sides. At each of these entrances are three broad flights of steps, of Finland granite, and each one of these flights of steps is cut from one solid block of granite, implying an enormous outlay of labor and expense. Indeed, the display of the products of Russia's quarries and mines of granite, malachite, porphyry, lapis lazuli, rhodonite, and other stones, as seen in the superb columns in this church, both within and without, strikes the visitor with wonder and amazement by their size, cutting, and exquisite finish.

Each of the great entrances to the cathedral has twenty-eight magnificent pillars supporting its portico, and each of these is sixty feet in height, seven feet in diameter; all are monoliths or single pieces of granite, perfectly round and beautifully polished and wrought. Their Corinthian capitals are of bronze, and uphold an enormous frieze of stone, above which is the ornamental pediment — that triangular part of the portico bounded by the edges of the roof; upon the point or summit of each of the pediments was a group of huge bronze figures. Recollect there are four of these grand entrances, each with pillars sixty feet high, with their Corinthian capitals and bases of bronze; one hundred and twelve pillars in all, as smooth as if made from run metal, and larger than those in the Pantheon at Rome.

In the pediments and at the angles and corners of the building are huge bronze figures of martyrs, saints, and apostles. The cupola which rises from the centre is two hundred and ninety-six feet in height, and, as I looked up at its great dome glittering with its golden covering, I counted the beautiful granite pillars up there that supported it, thirty in number, and just above them a circle of about that number of openings or windows; then came the glorious dome, and rising above it, flashing in the sunlight, was the huge gilded cross, at an altitude of three hundred and thirty-six feet above the ground. There are four smaller cupolas, at angles of the building, in which bells are placed.

The great bronze figures that adorn the pediments are eight feet high, and my guide stated that there were no fewer than sixty-three statues and fifty-one bas-reliefs, and nearly a hundred alto-relievo busts. The principal dome is built of iron, and is sixty-six feet in diameter. It is covered with copper and overlaid with gold, one hundred and eighty-five pounds (avoirdupois) of the precious metal being required for the gilding.

Round and round this architectural wonder and triumph you should go again and again to get a realizing sense of its wonderful proportions, to grasp it in your mind and carry away the never-to-be-forgotten impression that it creates, like St. Peter's at Rome. How this vast weight could be sustained upon the swampy soil of St. Petersburg is a wonder. It is said that myriads of piles, each twenty-one feet in length, were driven for its foundation, and at an expense of over a million of dollars. The whole building had cost, when completed, with its magnificent marble carvings and decorations, over fifteen millions of dollars. The cathedral was consecrated in 1858.

But if amazed at the grand proportions and simple architecture of the exterior, how much more is the visitor astonished by the splendor and wealth of the interior! It is a bewildering mass of magnificent marble, precious stones, gilding, and sumptuous carving and decoration. Ingenuity seems to have been exhausted in the elegant working of obdurate and stubborn stone into beautiful architectural proportions, and in presenting costly material in such abundance as to render its value, there at least, apparently insignificant.

There are great malachite pillars thirty feet high, huge columns of lapis lazuli worth thirty thousand dollars each, superb rhodonite work, a sort of rose-colored granite, and another the color of black lead, nearly as hard as iron, but susceptible of exquisite polish, and wrought so beautifully by the stone-cutters and sculptors that it looked like run metal.

The entire floors and walls of the cathedral are of the costliest and most elegant native marbles, of various colors; on every side, jasper, porphyry, and other valuable stone are wrought into the building from floor to ceiling. There is a small sanctuary or inner temple, which is a gorgeous affair, its beautiful dome being upheld by eight Corinthian pillars of malachite, each eight feet high. These pillars, my guide-book tells me, contain thirty-four thousand pounds of malachite, and cost twenty-five thousand pounds sterling.

The magnificent proportions of the great dome, the gorgeousness of the golden screen, or *iconastos*, which shuts off a sort of inner sanctuary for the priest, the superb mosaics and paintings, the blaze of many little candles before decorated shrines, the soft mellow twilight that pervades the interior, all combine to impress the beholder. Added to this, I was fortunate enough to arrive while service was going on, and heard some of that superb intoning, that marvellous bass singing, to be heard only in Russia. The priest who stood before the altar-screen had a wonderful voice; it was like that of a full-toned organ-pipe, and rang clear and musical, filling the building with its melody.

St. Isaac's was forty years in process of building, being completed in 1858, and its name is derived from a saint in the Greek liturgy, St. Isaac the Dalmatian, not the patriarch we read of in the Bible. The bell of this cathedral weighs fifty-three thousand pounds.

Dressed in a long black robe, with a sort of brimless, bell-crowned hat upon his head, the priest chanted, in deep, sonorous tones, a sort of service, which was taken up and repeated in a different key by eight or ten others, whose voices were in perfect unison, and sounded like an organ performance, as the notes resounded through the vast edifice; there was no musical accompaniment whatever.

There are no seats in Russian churches; the worshippers all stand when not kneeling. The poor people come in, and near the entrance purchase for a small fee one or two candles, about the size of a lead-pencil, of a priest who has them for sale. After lighting one, each goes to one of the shrines, that of his patron saint, — every Russian has one, — and, after bowing before it, lights his candle at the holy lamp, and sticks it in a large gilt or silvered frame placed there for that purpose. He then kneels or prostrates himself till his head touches the pavement, and there remains a short time, repeating his prayers, or rises to his knees and reverently crosses himself. The sale of wax candles seems to be quite a productive traffic for the church.

In departing from the churches, you find on each side of the porch, just outside, a line of begging nuns and monks, from four to twelve in number. These are authorized beggars, from different monasteries and nunneries. They stand with a prayer-book — open at a certain text, I suppose — or with a plate, in which is a bit of cloth, on which is embroidered a cross, and, as you pass by, smilingly solicit alms for their institutions. I was told that the begging nuns, after having obtained a certain sum, were comfortably supported during the remainder of their lives.

There are said to be about eight hundred convents in Russia. Abbots of some of the larger monasteries get an income, in some cases, of ten thousand pounds a year, and abbesses nearly as much. A large income is derived from the sale of holy relics, images, charms against sickness, holy tapers, and wedding rings. Russians of wealth, also, pay large sums for sepulture within monasteries, and most families of rank are buried within monasteries or churches.

The churches seem at all times to have a throng of worshippers, and each shrine, image, and chapel a group crossing themselves before it. The poorer people are very devout and very superstitious, and pay far more attention to their devotions and demonstrations of reverence than I have ever seen in Latin countries.

CHAPTER X.

THE poor, wretched, sheepskin-clad peasant that is spoken of by travellers one seldom sees in St. Petersburg, for that is the Paris of Russia; indeed, the accommodations at our hotel, and the general appearance of the interior of the large stores, reminded me of those in New York. Then, the broad and beautiful avenues, — there seemed to be no alleys or narrow streets, — the grand squares and magnificent piles of buildings ranging block after block in long lines on the Nevski Prospect and other great streets, and the grand public buildings astonished us, for so little has been written and said of them that it was a new revelation instead of the actual realization of others' descriptions.

The grand and splendidly built bridges over the river excited our admiration, and broad, well built quays with the lofty stone palaces and residences; but these, as well as the quays themselves, we were told, were not what they seemed, of solid stone, but imitations in stucco and plaster.

Of the interior of these imposing structures we had little opportunity of judging during our brief sojourn, but if they were on the scale as regards apartments that their exteriors indicated they must have been vast and magnificent. I was told that many of the Russian noblemen and men of wealth had banquet-halls, conservatories, and elegant winter gardens enclosed in their residences.

We started out behind our waiting steeds early one Sunday morning to see the "Cathedral of our Lady of Kazan," as it is called, going there first in preference to another church at which it was rumored the emperor would visit for his devotion, and on account of which the public would not be admitted until after twelve o'clock, noon. It is rarely that tourists, unless remaining at Petersburg for several days, get a good sight of the emperor; like all royal personages, his carriage is driven very rapidly through the streets, and his intended movements under the present state of affairs are not publicly known.

On our route we passed one of the entrances of the royal palace, about the door of which were lounging and waiting about twenty Cossacks of the royal guard, and upon the other side of the street a crowd awaiting the emperor, who was expected to come out at that portal — very likely to wait in vain, as our guide informed us many English and American tourists had done, this assemblage of guards being often a ruse designed to deceive as to the point at which he was likely to emerge. The string of guards, police and extraordinary precautions to guard the czar that we read of in the newspapers, we saw nothing of.

The Kazan Cathedral is on the Nevski Prospect, and any one who has seen St. Peter's at Rome at once recognizes the imitation of its colonnade of pillars. This church is built in the shape of a cross. It is 238 feet long from end to end of each bar of the cross, and 182 feet wide.

The interior is imposing and magnificent. As we drove up to one of the three grand entrances, our driver halted discreetly about a score of paces away from another carriage — like our own, except that a uniformed officer sat on the box, beside the driver, and a couple of mounted guards were near it. At first we thought the czar was to be the occupant, as we saw a tall uniformed figure emerge from the cathedral, but it proved to be the Grand Duke Michael, his uncle, who seated himself in the vehicle, drove directly past and within three or four yards of our carriage, courteously and smilingly returning our salute as he passed.

Upon entering the cathedral, we found but very few persons within, certainly not over twenty or thirty, who were lost in its immensity, and we considered ourselves fortunate, as there would be no service for two hours, in having abundance of time to inspect the interior. The view upwards into the great cupola, that rises 220 feet above the floor, is very fine; the cupola is supported by four huge pillars of Finland granite, and from each of these four pillars extends a row to the screen between nave and altar, and the three grand entrances of the church.

These pillars are monoliths, 56 in number and 35 feet in height. Like those of St. Isaac's, they rest on bases of solid bronze, and have Corinthian capitals of the same material. This church is named for Our Lady of Kazan, on account of a legend, that an image of the Virgin which it possesses was miraculously preserved amid the ashes of a conflagration of the old Tartar city of Kazan, about 1570, and brought to St. Petersburg about 1820.

We viewed the beautiful perspective views of the church at different points, and the groups of captured flags taken from Turkey, Persia, and France by the Russians, those of the latter being the historic French eagles captured from Napoleon during his memorable Russian campaign. There were also the huge keys of captured fortresses, suspended from the church pillars — among them those of Hamburg, Dresden, and Utrecht, also the captured bâton of Davoust, one of Napoleon's marshals, who earned his title of Prince, at the battle of Eckmühl, in one of the fiercest cavalry fights on record.

But the most wonderful thing here is the screen, — or *ikonastos*, as they call it, — a partition in Russian churches between the nave and the altar. This screen is made of solid silver, which was originally plundered from different Russian churches by the French, but was recaptured from them by the Cossacks, during the disastrous retreat from Moscow. Not only is the screen of silver, but so also is a balustrade in front of it. In the centre of the screen, the name of God is wrought in precious stones, and before it stand four huge solid silver candelabra.

By virtue of the persuasive powers of our guide, we enjoyed the largest liberty, and were permitted close examination of the wonderful portrait of the Virgin which is hung upon the screen. This picture, which is the usual portrait size, is entirely covered, with the exception of the face, with gold and precious stones of rare value, diamonds, rubies, emeralds, and sapphires, one huge one of the latter description being that presented by a grand-duchess. This altar-screen and its surroundings were one blaze of gold, silver, and gems, and in such abundance as to cause them to appear as if but of comparatively small value, for it seemed almost incredible that real stones should be distributed so plentifully and lavishly as they were here. But they were real, nevertheless.

As we were standing near to and closely inspecting this jewelled wonder, a bell rang violently behind the screen. Pilley, our guide, rushed to us, and, in startled tones, said: —

"Come away quickly as you can! Here comes the emperor!"

We stood not upon the order of our going, and had scarcely got outside the rail ere the tall figure of the emperor, followed by the empress, passed in and on to a position in front of the jewelled picture, where they knelt for perhaps five minutes, and, let us suppose, said a prayer or two.

Standing some thirty paces away, where our guide had pulled us, and not having the "dread and fear of kings," I determined upon having a nearer view of His Majesty, and therefore approached to within ten paces of the silver rail, opposite the point of exit. Rising from his knees, the emperor advanced with a rapid step, and, catching sight of us, recognized our salutation by a courteous bow, a pleasant smile, and a raising of his hand to his helmet cap. He wore a gray military overcoat, cavalry sabre, riding-boots with spurs, and a military helmet cap, like the Russian helmet except that it lacked the projecting spike on the crown. His form was broad, heavy, and stalwart, and he had the air of a coarse, overfed man, stout but not fat with good living. He walked at an ordinary gait, bowing now and then in response to the salutes of the few persons in the church, and, as he passed out, we heard the shouts of the people, as his carriage drove away.

The empress was habited in a close-fitting dress of dark green cloth, a dark bonnet and lace mask veil, and, from the hasty glimpse we caught of her, seemed quite a pretty woman. Not a single guard or attendant came in with the royal pair or escorted them out;

from the door to the altar-screen they were utterly without attendants, and we might easily in a dozen paces have crossed their path or intercepted them, for there certainly appeared to be no one to have prevented our so doing.

Our guide congratulated us upon our rare good-fortune in obtaining this near view of His Majesty with so little trouble; it was, he declared, an unusual occurrence, and tourists generally counted themselves fortunate who saw him at a distance, as he rapidly drove through the streets of the city. It certainly upset all my preconceived ideas of caution on the part of the czar, who, I supposed, would have been guarded by a double line of soldiers, and every one excluded from the church in which he made his devotions.

There is so much to claim the attention of the sight-seer and tourist in St. Petersburg that an attempt to see all thoroughly would occupy many months' time, and a description thereof occupy many hundreds of pages. This, I presume, accounts for what appear to be the very meagre descriptions that we find have been thus far given of the wonders of the Russian capital.

I can give but passing mention of the magnificent Winter Palace, which is the residence of the emperor and court during the winter season. This building is 450 feet in length by 350 in width, and during the court season is occupied by six thousand persons. The palace contains superb galleries of paintings, chiefly representations of Russian victories and portraits of celebrated Russian generals. Its great audience-chamber is an apartment 140 feet long and 60 feet wide. Other notable rooms are Peter the Great's throne-room and the beautiful White Saloon, so called from its decorations of pure white and gold. The grand staircase is another feature, and among the wonders that the tourist must not miss are the Russian crown-jewels, including the Orloff diamond, which weighs $194\frac{3}{4}$ carats and is said to be the largest in the world.

The vast national museum, known as the Hermitage, like the British Museum or the Vatican, is of such extent that the tourist wonders if he can carry away a correct impression of any portion of it, in the all too brief period which his sojourn, be it even one of weeks, allows him.

The Hermitage was founded by that remarkable woman, Catherine the Great, and was designed by her as a place of retirement from the cares of state, and where she might receive men of letters, great artists, sculptors, and philosophers. Here she proposed to gather together specimens of the works of great artists, and to rival the collections in the great European capitals and in the art galleries. The work which she began has been faithfully carried out, as the traveller who visits them will see for himself that the collections of Rome, Florence, and Paris are dwarfed by it.

Here is a collection of magnificent pictures, one of the finest in Northern Europe; for here may be seen fine examples of Teniers, Rubens, Guido, Rembrandt, Velasquez, Carlo Dolci, Van Dyck, Snyders, Correggio, and many other celebrated masters. The building is a great parallelogram, 515 by 375 feet, with a magnificent entrance. A vestibule upheld by ten caryatides, twelve or fifteen feet high, cut from granite, with statues of sculptors: artists and painters are placed in niches, and you enter a great hall supported by the usual beautiful colonnade of pillars, cut from Finland granite.

The picture galleries are arranged for different

schools of art. For instance, one is devoted to the Italian school, in which the superb picture of the "Dispute of the Doctors," by Guido Reni, and his "David with the Head of Goliath," figure, the " Feast of Cleopatra," by Tiepolo, " St. Cecilia," by Carlo Dolci, and scores of others, each one of which is a feast to the art-lover. In this hall were four large candelabra, of beautiful violet jasper. Russia seems to be the home of elegant and precious stones, and of workmen who rival the old sculptors in their skill of carving them. Another large hall is filled with works of Flemish artists, a third with those of the Spanish school, another with works of French artists, and another contains an English collection.

The numerous examples of the works of great artists strike the inexperienced traveller, visiting Russia for the first time, and who has a vague idea that he has left artistic collections behind him on crossing the frontier, with astonishment. For instance, here is one room full of beautiful specimens from Raphael's pencil, sixty in number, and another containing his frescos, another with several fine Titians, another full of Potter, Teniers, and Wouvermans, some of the best of the last-named artist's I ever saw, and one, as our guide-book truly informed us, without the usual white horse. Then, besides these are beautiful Rembrandts, Rubenses, Gerard Dows, Correggios, great pictures of fruit and game by Snyders, twenty fine Murillos, over thirty Van Dycks, and many others I cannot recall, to say nothing of the beautiful collection of the works of artists of more modern date, of the German, French, and Russian schools. Nowhere except in Spain is there such a fine exposition of Spanish art as is exhibited in these galleries.

Two of Canova's most famous statues — the "Dancing Girl" and "Hebe"— stand at the head of a marble staircase in the Hermitage.

The Emperor of Russia had, at the time of the author's visit, just purchased the famous Gallitzin collection of pictures, for the Hermitage Gallery, the price being one hundred and twenty thousand pounds. The Gallitzin collection, which is one of the finest in Russia, was principally purchased in Germany and Italy, during the early part of the present century. The gem of the gallery is one of the two Crucifixions painted by Raphael in his early days, which was long attributed to Perugino. The other Crucifixion by Raphael, belonging to the same period, is at Dudley House, having been bought in Italy by the late Lord Dudley.

But, besides the wealth of pictorial art, there is much else in the Hermitage to claim the attention, and it is a pity that no popular exposition in the English language of the contents of this wonderful museum has yet been published. Its archæological collection appears to be one of great value and interest: the results of the excavations at Kertch; the collection of Greek vases is a superb one; the numismatic collection is quite large, including a splendid series of the coinage of Russia.

Archæologists find the collection from the excavations of Kertch to be the most unique and extraordinary in existence. Kertch was the ancient Panticapæum, one of the chief Greek colonies of the Euxine, and the excavations and discoveries made by the explorers of the Russian government have brought forth a collection of beautiful goldsmithery and antique vases that exceeds in extent that of any museum in Europe.

The gold-work is of various races and ages. The earliest Greek examples date from about the fifth century B. C.; and there is a quantity of curious Scythian work, that defies exact chronology.

The splendor and delicacy of some of the gold work is wonderful, when we consider the age in which it was produced, and the visitor finds not a meagre or even moderate collection to study, but is fairly bewildered among the numerous cases of gold bracelets and necklaces, ear-rings, finger-rings, buckles, figures of animals, crowns of gold-leaf, silver vases, chains, charms, and ornaments of all kinds. There was a splendid pair of gold ear-rings, bearing the head of a goddess, beautifully executed, the head, hair, face, and ornaments of the head all superbly wrought, and in a manner that a workman of to-day might feel proud of, and yet it was made in the fifth century B. C.

Then, there were beautifully wrought necklaces, one ornamented with figures of beasts, and another with a delicately interlaced pattern covered with gold-dust, the style of which modern jewellers have striven in vain to imitate. Curious ancient silver-work, including beautifully ornamented vases, are placed here, and belong, I am told, to the Sassanian period, and furnish partial explanation of the origin of Arab and Mesopotamian metal work.

Among the Grecian antiquities was a helmet, exactly such a one as we see in the illustrated books of the stories of the old Greek heroes, and the curious thing respecting this helmet is that the head of the owner is still with it, and was found in it. The copper head-piece was not proof, however, against the tremendous force with which it was hit, evidently by a stone from a sling, judging from the smashed-in fracture, which bent the metal like paper, and cracked the skull of the wearer likewise, as that remnant of mortality shows to-day. Another interesting object is the sarcophagus of a young man; upon the sides of this is beautifully sculptured the story of his life as a student and young man, showing his resistance of temptation, and his advancement in wisdom and scholarship. As one looks upon the artistic beauty of such work, even after time had wrought its work of so many years upon it, he cannot help imagining what a city of artistic splendor the ancient Grecian capital must have been in its time, and doubting if much advancement in artistic skill has been made since.

The Russian government is prosecuting discoveries far north of the Ural Mountains, and near Samarcand, and has an unparalleled collection of other antiquities displayed here, such as rude Tartar silver-work, early Russian *cloisonné* enamels, gold bracelets with Arabic inscriptions, and curious Græco-Scythic terra-cotta ware dug up at Samarcand. There is also a collection of three thousand Greek vases, many bearing beautiful designs, such as ships, animals, and chariots; some of the finest of these are of the seventh century B. C. The numismatic collection is very large, and must be of immense value; the Russian and oriental sections are the most remarkable; the oriental, I was told, numbers over eight thousand pieces, among which is the splendid gold indemnity that was paid by the Shah of Persia after the war of 1828; it also includes some curious pieces of great weight.

There are over two hundred thousand specimens in the entire collection, and one of the most interesting portions of it is the section devoted to the coins of ancient Greece and Rome, with which are displayed several hundred curious Athenian coins. Among the curiosities of this collection are some rough junks of silver, a quarter of a pound each, the "roubles" of the fifteenth century, and the square copeck and half-copeck of iron.

A most interesting collection is one contained in three cases of ancient English coins. Only think of finding in a Russian museum a collection of coins of the reigns of the English kings Ethelred II., Canute, and Hardicanute! Certainly this collection is most remarkable, and one that, I should judge, numismatists would find to contain many rare and even unique specimens.

CHAPTER XI.

PETER THE GREAT is canonized as a saint. He seems to be considered almost a god by the lower order of Russians; the peasants rub their foreheads in the dirt before the house he lived in, and bow and cross themselves before his pictures with the same reverence they bestow upon saints of the church. Peter was one of the heroes of our school-boy days; one of the principal figures in our story-books, and the prominent one in the meagre sketch of Russia given in school histories, his cruelty and tyranny being carefully kept out of sight. So we were curious to see, and glad to have opportunity of inspecting closely, the relics of this remarkable man, preserved in one of the rooms of the Hermitage. We grasped in our hands the iron rod he was said to have used as a walking-stick, saw the wax cast taken from his face while living, took in hand the mathematical instruments that he used, saw the clothes that he wore, the turning-lathe and carving-tools, and specimens of engraving on copper executed by him, a notched stick, showing Peter's height to be six feet eight inches, that of his valet seven feet, and many other interesting relics.

Peter unquestionably did more than any other monarch to advance Russia in civilization. Possessing enormous power of endurance, perseverance, and great versatility, he appears to have acted under the impression that, under his direction and force of will, Russia could gain or advance in his reign to the point that it had taken other nations hundreds of years to attain.

It is a wonder to see what mechanical work this monarch made himself master of, and what he accomplished was so very far in advance of his time in his own country that we cannot cease to wonder at it. He built and navigated his own boat, translated works into Russian, learned the carpenter's trade, how to engrave on copper, built navies, and erected the first schools in Russia to teach arithmetic.

After passing Peter the Great's room, we came to another, in which was a wonderful collection of snuff-boxes, such as would have made the eyes of a virtuoso or collector sparkle with delight. They were chiefly the gifts of sovereigns, and were resplendent with jewels, or adorned with beautifully painted miniatures of their donors, or monograms and ciphers in precious stones. Following still further this wonderful museum, the visitor finds case after case of the most elegant and costly bric-à-brac and jewelry, till the brain is weary, and the limbs fatigued, in endeavoring to give even a cursory glance at them.

For instance, there is a whole case of curious watches, Nuremberg eggs, watches shaped like ducks, and other quaint conceits; a case of carved ivory work; the silver and gold toys of Catherine II.; caskets covered with great pearls and precious stones; plumes made of diamonds and other gems; crystal cups covered with diamonds; huge silver goblets, elaborately engraved; bouquets of flowers, formed entirely of emeralds, rubies, sapphires, and other precious stones; Dresden china ornamented with diamonds; cups of rock-crystal; superb ivory carved work; Chinese jade work; gold and silver filigree work, a large and curious collection; then a case holding a collection of curious and historic finger-rings.

I am giving but the briefest glance at this wonderful array of curios, before which the celebrated Green Vaults of Dresden, wonderful as they are, are fairly dwarfed.

Among the droll but at the same time interesting collections was a great case full of curious and historic pocket-books! Here was one ornamented with diamonds and rubies, that belonged to the wife of Frederick William the Great; another of King Augustus of Poland; another that was given to the first queen of Prussia, by Peter the Great. Verily, if any artful dodger could have stolen one of these pocket-books, it would have been a rich haul, even though not "lined," as Fagin expressed it.

After all this lavish display of fanciful work, the collection of gems, although one of the largest in existence, seems tame till one begins to examine the beautiful designs and the antique and wonderful cutting displayed.

This collection is one of the largest in existence. Among them I remember a superb ruby, four inches long, cut into a bust of Peter the Great.

Library and sculpture gallery are included within this great museum, which might occupy weeks of one's time, had he it to spare, but from which I emerged with a handful of guide-books, and a chaotic impression of pictures, diamonds, emeralds, snuff-boxes, coins, rich antiques, rare vases, curious relics, wonderful antiquities, and rich rarities, such as it is seldom the lot of man to look upon, and this, too, in what previous impressions had led me to believe was the least likely country in which to find them. And here let me say that, without such a guide as James Pilley, whom we took care to engage for our entire stay, I doubt whether we could have seen one-half that we saw, gained admission to half the places of interest that we did, or have comprehended what we did see so thoroughly as he made us through his skilful guidance.

The man deserves mention as quite a remarkable personage in many respects, especially as compared with the various *valets de places* I have encountered and employed in various other countries.

An Englishman, he has lived and been a guide thirty years in Russia, speaks the language fluently, and appears to be personally acquainted with every custodian in Petersburg, Moscow, and Nijni. He shakes hands with head-priests and nuns, is greeted by abbots and lady superiors, knows officers, policemen, janitors, and door-keepers, and, moreover, understands how to economize time and keep his party hard at work every moment. I think he rather enjoyed having two men that did not tire down with day after day of sight-seeing, — *i. e.*, during the day, — but, after an all-day work of eight or ten hours or more, it did, after a while, seem rather a test of endurance for this indefatigable man to call, after he had allowed us an hour and a half for dinner, and say the carriage was "ready for the evening concert garden, gentlemen — carriage is engaged for all day, gentlemen, up to midnight." After one or two evening excursions, however, we gave our guide and driver the benefit of the time that was ours after 7 P. M., for the reason that rest was absolutely necessary.

Besides a good guide, assuming that you get a good one, who is reasonably honest, let the tourist not stint him, if any pinch comes, for a bribe or *douceur* where it will be of service. This, in Russia, procures much very desirable and prompt service, and also some quite important privileges, as I shall show further on.

We found no difficulty on account of any stringent police regulations, which we had reason to expect from various published accounts of travellers who have got into difficulties. It may be because our guide thoroughly arranged matters for us, or because the much-talked-of espionage as regards foreigners, especially Americans, does not now exist in the large Russian cities. Our guide laughed at some of the stories that we rehearsed to him, and, on inquiry as to any line of conduct, remarked that one had only to behave like a gentleman, as he would in any other large city, and not deliberately break the laws of the land, and no difficulties would be experienced.

It might be as well not to be too outspoken on political matters, and especially in condemning the government and advocating revolutionary measures, in mixed company or public places. A curious case was related to me of an adventure which occurred a few years ago here to an American traveller, who, with that freedom of speech which characterizes some of our countrymen in foreign countries, was especially bitter in his condemnation of the policy of the Russian government. Not only this, but, in the matter of regulations at places of interest which he visited, he did not hesitate to find fault without scruple or reserve.

Just after he had finished dinner one day, the landlord of the hotel, pale and trembling, came to him with the intelligence that a messenger of the police desired to see him. On repairing to the next room, he was greeted in English, with but a slight accent, by a gentlemanly-appearing individual, who said:—

" I have the honor to address Mr. Blank?"

"That is my name."

"I have the honor to be the bearer of your passport, and also to state that the train leaves for the German frontier to-morrow morning, at half-past eight o'clock."

"But I am not going by that train! I intend visiting Moscow."

"That will be impossible."

"Impossible! Why?"

"Because I have special orders to escort Monsieur to the frontier."

"You have orders! I want no escort. What if I refuse?"

"But you will not refuse, I am certain, when I inform you I act by the orders of the imperial police!"

"The imperial police!"

"Certainly. The utmost courtesy will be shown Mr. Blank if he promptly complies and is ready with his baggage at eight o'clock to-morrow morning. If he refuses, why — (shrugging his shoulders) — but I know Mr. Blank will be too wise to refuse."

And the officer bowed himself out, without a glance at the landlord, who stood in one corner, a mute witness of the interview.

After listening to that individual's explanations as to the probable cause of this expulsion, and the consequences of a refusal to obey the order of the police, the American concluded the better part of valor was discretion, and was ready with his luggage at the time appointed, when his caller of the previous evening appeared promptly with a drosky, and both drove to the railroad station.

Nor did they part here. A comfortable compartment on the train was placed at the American's disposal, while his companion took seat in an adjoining one, and he soon found the Russian was one vested in authority, from the deference which was paid to him by railroad officials along the route.

He was affable and polite, and conversed fluently, carefully avoiding any reference to politics. In reply to the query as to why he was escorting his charge, and how the latter had offended, he replied that it was only his duty to carry out the commands of his superior officers, and he must beg to be excused explanations.

The American was sensible enough to press the matter no further, and found his custodian quite an agreeable companion, and his cigars unexceptionable.

Arrived at the frontier, on dismounting, the official politely remarked to his charge that at this point it would be necessary for him to purchase a ticket for the remainder of the journey, and that here also he had the honor to present his adieux, with best wishes for a safe journey to Berlin. He then handed the traveller his passport, which was endorsed with certain Russian characters, and, after the ticket was procured, bowed him into the train, courteously waving his white handkerchief to his late prisoner, as he sped away.

The latter, in telling the story, is said to have remarked, with true American satisfaction, that he "got a free pass to the frontier out of the Russian government, anyhow."

One of the most remarkable exhibitions we visited in St. Petersburg was the Museum of Imperial Carriages, a wonderful collection of rich and curious vehicles. Besides the carriages, the rooms contain a splendid collection of Gobelin tapestry, suspended upon the walls, which alone is worth a visit. Here is one splendid but rather cumbersome vehicle, sent by Frederick the Great to the Empress Elizabeth, a magnificently decorated affair, rich in gilding and splendid upholstery, the arms of Russia on the panels in imitation and real precious stones, but not the most valuable, and surmounted with the imperial crown. Several elegant vehicles are more or less connected with the history of that luxurious Empress, Catherine II. One made in England for her has the driver's box upheld by carved and gilded eagles, its panels beautifully painted with representations of allegorical subjects, exquisitely done, while on the outside and back are representations of Apollo and the Muses. Another is richly lined with lace, and the panels adorned by beautiful pictures by Gravelot — of Venus bathing, and other subjects; another, on which gilding, velvet, and imitation precious stones seem to have been exhausted in decorating even to the steps, is also ornamented with paintings on its panels, any one of which would be a valuable addition to a picture gallery. These grand carriages are all brought out at each coronation at Moscow, when they are carefully put in order and restored for the occasion.

But, amid all this collection of richly gilded vehicles, which suggests, to the average American, the " Golden Chariot" of the circus, the object that attracts the most attention is the sledge built by Peter the Great, with his own hands — indeed, we begin to wonder if there was any species of industry this remarkable monarch did not turn his hands to. The vehicle alluded to is rather a clumsy affair, like a small hut, with mica windows, and has a box behind it for clothes and provisions.

The carriage of Alexander II., with the back part all split and shivered by the Nihilist bomb from which he escaped only to be killed after descending therefrom is here, and a reminder and relic of that affair. Still a stronger reminder which we saw is the pavement spattered with his blood, and his sword and other articles bearing the same gory stains, that have been preserved, near the very spot where he fell, in a small temporary temple erected over them, and guarded by a priest, who receives offerings from the faithful, who stop there to pray, in aid of a church which is to be raised on the spot to his memory.

Stepping into an adjoining apartment, we found it to be a harness and livery room, containing the richly mounted harnesses for all these equipages, and the liveries of nearly a thousand men. All the harness, wherever metal is used, is of silver. The reins are of silver thread and silk. A huge heap of old harness trimmings, a bushel or two of what I took to be plated metal, I was told was solid silver, and so I found it to be on examination, silver that had been taken from old harnesses to be refitted, the metal to go to the melting pot. These royal people seem to deal in gold and silver by the bushel, and diamonds by the quart.

The imperial stables, near by, are a vast extent of buildings, accommodating nearly five hundred carriage and saddle horses. Murray says: "They will give an idea of the magnificence of the Russian court, as the sum expended in feeding the horses alone is about ten thousand pounds per annum."

A most interesting place to visit is the Academy of Sciences, an institution founded in 1724, and which contains various collections of great interest and importance, and a library of nearly two hundred thousand volumes and MSS.; among the books are about fourteen hundred in the Chinese language, and nearly ten thousand in various dialects of the East.

The zoölogical collection is perhaps the most interesting department to foreign visitors. It certainly was to me, for here I saw the unfossilized remains of the gigantic mastodon that I had read and wondered at as one of the wonders of modern times, as it certainly is, being one of the relics of that age of the world, far back in the antediluvian era, that the geologists tell of.

The skeletons of the great rhinoceros and mastodon are wonderful remains, and more wonderful from the fact that when they were discovered, it will be recollected, they were encased in Siberian ice, where they had been preserved for countless ages, and so perfectly preserved that, when revealed by the breaking-away of the ice-cliff, when they were discovered, in 1806, the bears and wolves came to feed on the flesh that had been preserved for centuries from decay.

The skeleton of this mastodon, although over ten feet high and about fifteen in length, was that of a young beast, for the entire leg-bones of others that were afterwards found dwarf this, as it in turn does the skeleton of an elephant set up by its side for comparison. The huge skull of another mammoth, one-third larger than the one on the entire skeleton, also shows that the latter is the remains of a youngster. Some of the mammoth tusks exhibited here are eight and one-half feet in length. A large section of the skin taken from this mammoth is preserved, and still has the reddish-brown hair upon it that distinguished the animal in northern latitudes.

A capital restoration of this enormous creature, with tusks, hide, hair, etc., all carefully reproduced complete, under the direction of skilled naturalists, was exhibited, in 1885, at the International Exposition at New Orleans.

Scarcely of less interest were the remains of a huge species of extinct rhinoceros, upon the head of which still remain the skin and hair, which also still adhere to the feet. Science has even been able, by analyzing the particles found in the cavities of the teeth of this huge beast, to determine that its food was the branches of young fir-trees. Other fragments of the great beasts of early periods will interest the scientific student.

One curious feature of the collection was the Ethnographic Department, which was an exposition of the dresses, arms, implements, etc., of the various races that are under the Russian government, an assortment of wonderful weapons, costumes, and household goods, that was a museum of itself. Bows and arrows, spears and battle-axes, primitive war-clubs, and the chain armor, and decorated Eastern helmets, figures clad in mere skins, and the gay costumes of Circassian soldiers, head-dresses of peasants, and the bone ornaments of the savage were displayed, and formed a rare and interesting object-lesson respecting the extent and diversity of territory and people under the sway of the Russian sceptre.

The collection of coins here shows the regular progress of coinage in Russia from the earliest period, when stamped leather passed current, down to the bright gold pieces of the present day.

The mineralogical collection shows the wonderful mineral resources of the empire, and the anatomical cabinet contains many wonderful curiosities in medical science, of interest not only to the pathological student, but to the ordinary visitor who wishes to be astonished by the monstrosities and curiosities of humanity.

The skeleton of Peter the Great's valet, who was seven feet in height, is preserved here, and the head of a favorite mistress of Peter is also shown, not a very attractive object now. One must, of course, not leave St. Petersburg without seeing all the relics of Peter the Great, and everything that specially relates to him. He will find them in every direction — in museum, church, palace, and monastery. In one of the great squares, known as Admiralty Square, stands his equestrian statue, so well known from pictorial representations. It is a spirited and beautiful production, and, like many other celebrated foreign works of art that I had read and heard of, fully came up to my ideal of the reality.

The attitude is bold and spirited, but is one which is also used in other similar works, the equestrian statue of Jackson, for instance, at Washington, although the latter has nothing like the graceful pose, nor the figure the ease and majestic grace of that of the Russian group.

The huge rock that forms the pedestal of this statue is in itself a wonder; it is of granite, weighing fifteen hundred tons, and was brought from a point four or five miles distant from the city, by means of rollers and other contrivances, with an infinite deal of labor and expense.

A story is told of a couple of American sailors who, while out on a frolic, invaded the sacred precincts of this statue, and the bolder of the two climbed, not only upon the pedestal, but upon the bronze horse, and seated himself behind the figure of the great czar, and was waving his hat in triumph when he was pounced upon and borne off by the police. Next day before the magistrate, through his captain and the American consul's intervention, he was let off on condition that he paid a fine of three hundred roubles.

It was remonstrated that the fine was a large one for so small an offence. "Quite the contrary," replied the magistrate; "he who would ride with emperors must pay accordingly."

Not far from here, on the other side of the cathedral, stands a most elaborate equestrian statue of the Emperor Nicholas, he that was on the throne at the time of the Crimean War. In addition to the figure of the emperor are life-size figures, those of the empress and her three daughters, which are placed at each corner of the pedestal. In artistic finish and elaborate work this far excels the other, and is a superb and costly affair. But that of Peter, in its grand and spirited attitude and simplicity of surrounding, leaves a more lasting impression.

The cathedral founded by Peter the Great, known as the Cathedral of St. Peter and St. Paul, is named after him and also the Emperor Paul, who is buried there; it is within what is known as the fortification or fortress. Its spire is, as usual, surmounted by a cross, that glitters in the sunlight three hundred and seventy-one feet above the street — ten feet higher than St. Paul's of London.

The dome also shines with gilding. All the sovereigns of Russia, with the exception of Peter II., are buried here, many of them noted for their barbarous cruelty — deeds that make one shudder to read of. Even Peter himself, with all his ability and his advanced mind, that brought Russia so far from semi-barbarism to a civilized nation, was guilty of crimes that were a disgrace to humanity. Within the very fortress in which this cathedral stands, he imprisoned his oldest son, put him to torture under examination for treason; from the effect of this treatment he died soon after his father left him.

The bodies of the royal rulers are deposited under the floor of the cathedral, and the spot of the interment is marked by a stone sarcophagus above each. That of Peter the Great is opposite a statue of St. Peter, *i. e.*, Peter the Great canonized, and an inscription states that he was "nineteen inches long and five inches and a quarter broad at the time of his birth." A similar image of the Emperor Paul (as St. Paul) opposite his tomb gives his length and breadth at birth, and a long row of other tombs of Pauls. Alexis', Nicholas', and Constantine's may be studied by those familiar with Russian history.

That which interested us most, next to Peter's, was the grave of that wonderful, ambitious, and sensual woman, Catherine II., whose reign forms some of the most interesting pages of Russian history — a woman who, after living a life of unrestrained licentiousness, made her reign remarkable for the rapid increase of the extent and power of Russia, and the vigor and ability with which she carried on the government, and made her court noted by literati and philosophers of France, whom she invited there, many of whom did not hesitate to flatter and exalt her, notwithstanding her utter and open shamelessness in vice.

There is a splendid monument to Catherine, which was erected as late as 1873, on the Nevski Prospect, in front of the Alexander Theatre. It is a figure of the empress, upon a great pedestal of red granite, surrounded by statues of various distinguished Russians of her reign. The monument is eighty feet high, and cost half a million dollars.

The interior of the Peter and Paul church is decorated with standards taken from the Turks, French, and Swedes, which are placed upon the walls, and the ponderous keys of various captured fortresses.

From here we went to Peter the Great's cottage, which he lived in, on the banks of the Neva, while he was superintending the building of St. Petersburg. It is a little house about fifty feet by twenty, containing three rooms, and is entirely covered by a casing, to protect it from decay and relic-hunters. Of course, the principal room has been fitted up as a chapel, with an image which Peter used to carry about on his military campaigns, before which is a cross and holy water, and the crowd of pious Russians was too great for us to gain admission there. But in another room we saw the bench and chair upon which he sat, a boat that he built and used for his excursions across the river, and other articles that belonged to him.

Near here is an extensive parade-ground, or Champ de Mars, where troops, both foot and cavalry, are drilled and exercised. It is a vast square area, in which twenty thousand troops can be manœuvred at once.

We next visited his Summer Palace — in fact, his first state residence. A modest residence enough it seems now, about as large as a moderate country-house in America, its reception and ball-room being but little larger than great old-fashioned drawing-rooms, and his dining-room communicating directly with the rather small-looking kitchen by means of a slide in the wall. The cramped quarters and rude conveniences for cooking would hardly serve to stew and boil and roast for people of very moderate means of to-day.

The monastery of St. Alexander Nevski, at one end of the Nevski Prospect, we were fortunate enough to visit during a singing or chanting service of the monks — a wonderful specimen of vocalization. The monks wear long beards, and their long, light hair is crimped. The beard and hair are said to be worn in imitation of those of our Saviour. This monastery is in large and beautiful enclosed grounds, with church, monastery, and other buildings, and where, as far as we could see, the occupants lived most comfortably. The grounds are celebrated as being the battle-field where the Grand-Duke Alexander defeated the Swedes, in 1241. The church and monastery were not built, however, till five hundred years after.

The church, which is one of the largest in St. Petersburg, is finely decorated with marble fittings, gilding, and precious stones; but the principal attraction is the tomb of Alexander, which stands in a side chapel, which is of solid silver to the amount of three thousand two hundred and fifty pounds of the precious metal. It is surmounted by a catafalque, with angels five or six feet in height, blowing their trumpets, while numerous bass-reliefs represent scenes in Alexander's life. The value of the silver alone as raw material in this monument is over one hundred thousand dollars. The church and convent were founded by Peter the Great. In the cloister, they show you the crown of St. Alexander and the bed on which Peter the Great died, besides a collection of pontifical robes, mitres, and staffs of unexampled richness.

One peculiarity of the Russian churches, to which allusion has before been made, is the arrangement of the altar and screen, or *iconastos*, as it is called. There is a rail separating the steps leading to the altar; at the top of these steps the officiating priest stands when performing a portion of the service. Behind him is the screen, always richly and superbly decorated with gold, silver, or precious stones. In this screen are three doors, the middle one being the Holy Door. After passing behind the screen, you find the Holy Table — really the altar, I suppose, as I saw no such altars as in Roman Catholic churches. Above this table are a canopy, upheld by four small pillars, and a dove, as the symbol of the Holy Ghost. Beyond and fronting this table is an elegant raised seat or throne, upon which no official below the rank of a bishop is allowed to sit.

There are no seats in Russian churches. Everybody stands, except when kneeling at some particular part of the service, or when some are prostrating themselves, as many, especially of the poorer class, do, before some saint's picture or shrine, or even in the midst of a crowded congregation, should the spirit move them, at any time, to do so.

I have spoken of the begging nuns that stand just inside the doors of all the churches; they are a curiously costumed set, with high pointed hoods and different cuts of robes — according to the nunnery they represent, I suppose. Outside the porch, as in Roman Catholic countries, is the usual swarm of other beggars.

The beautiful miniature palace, a short ride from St. Petersburg, known as "Mine Own," and owned, I think, by the empress, is in the middle of some charmingly laid-out grounds, and awaits the royal family whenever they should please to come to it; but it had not been occupied by them for more than a year when we visited it. Its rooms are all fitted with exquisite taste, and without that tawdry and lavish display of gilt and frescoing that distinguishes royal palaces. Indeed, this was like the residence of a gentleman of perfect taste and abundant means.

An attempt to keep intelligible memoranda or to describe the endless display of riches and splendor in these Russian palaces and churches is futile, unless one should make a business of it, like cataloguing for an auction sale, and even then life would be too short for the task.

Those who visit Russia for the first time, with the somewhat popular idea that it is a sort of semi-barbaric country, and that most of the wealth and art of the world is held in other portions of Europe, are simply astounded with the wonders and treasures of St. Petersburg and Moscow. It must be remembered, however, that Russia has had the treasures of the East for years to draw upon, to say nothing of her mines and quarries, which are unsurpassed in richness and extent.

Not only is the tourist and pleasure-seeker who has visited London, Paris, Berlin, and Rome surprised at the novelties that he encounters, the wealth of art, and the wonderful beauty of churches and public buildings that he sees, but that more popular descriptions have not been given, and better guide-books written of the country and the people.

Russian novelists just now, however, are the fashion in American literary circles, and information about this great nation and its people will on that account be more sought for and more generally disseminated than ever before. There are only about six hundred periodicals of all kinds published in the Russian empire, of which two hundred are in other languages than Russian. In other words, it takes one hundred and seventy-five thousand Russian subjects to support one periodical, while in the United States there is one periodical to every four thousand people. Of the four hundred Russian periodicals, fifty-five are daily, eighty-five weekly. Much of our information respecting Russia has come through English sources, and has been tinctured by prejudice and marred by misrepresentations, as the author found from personal experience in many respects.

Besides this, many changes have been made for the better as regards the privileges of travellers, within a few years. The accounts of the perplexities of passports, surveillance of police, and rigorous regulations respecting tourists must have been greatly modified, or are customs of the past, as we experienced very little inconvenience in that respect.

The palace of Peterhof, is fairly crammed with room after room of rich articles of bric-à-brac, such as vases, silver statuettes, porcelain paintings of battles, carvings of ivory, and also, of course, including some carvings by Peter the Great, whose handiwork seems ubiquitous in and about Petersburg. One of the great rooms has over eight hundred portraits of females of different provinces of the Russian empire. These were painted by order of Catherine II., who commissioned an artist to travel over the empire, and obtain them from the best peasant models he could secure.

The drives and grounds round and about Peterhof, as well as the immediate vicinity, are charming. In front of the palace, a fountain sends a jet of water, with a mighty rush, eighty feet into the air, and on either side are other fountains, throwing their jets in different directions. Down at the foot of the elevated ground upon which the palace stands are great basins and other fountains, the water of which flows away through an artificial channel, lined on each side with smaller fountains. The rides about the grounds, which are elegantly laid out, continually bring you in view of most charming effects of fountains, basins, trees, and landscape.

But near a place called Marly is a magnificent fountain, in the shape of a Greek temple, in the middle of a lake, with streams of water spouting from various parts of it, flashing in the light in every direction. All around in the vicinity were lesser fountains, and artificially contrived water-works in such variety that I left the grounds of Peterhof and Marly with a confused impression of great foaming waves dashing over marble steps before a grand palace, or jets and streams leaping high as the tree-tops in broad avenues, or spouting from the mouths of Tritons or dolphins and splashing into marble basins in shady nooks, which met us at every fresh turn in these magnificent parks.

The favorite royal residence of the Russian imperial family is known as the Summer Palace, and is situated about fifteen miles from St. Petersburg by rail. After riding into the grounds, we passed by the front of this palace, seven hundred and eighty feet in length, profusely ornamented with columns, vases, statues, and other ornaments. It was originally covered with gilding, but is now white, except that portion towards the garden, which is painted a greenish hue. A detailed description of this royal palace, somewhat celebrated for being a favorite abiding-place of Catherine II., would be but a repetition of that of other Russian royal palaces.

The private chapel of the royal family which we visited in the palace is an elegant affair, richly decorated in blue and gold, the ceiling completely covered with gilding. The places for the royal family are in a sort of organ-loft or gallery, at one end of the chapel, opposite the screen (not even royalty can sit in church), where they can see all without being themselves exposed to view, and direct communication is had from this gallery to apartments in the palace. Some of these rooms are so rich and wonderful in decoration that I cannot pass them without brief mention.

The most wonderful is that known as the amber room, a large apartment, the walls, furniture, and decorations of which are entirely composed of amber. Dark yellow, delicate gold tint, and beautiful translucent straw color, of the rarest description, were bestowed here with Russian prodigality. The walls were sheathed with it, chandeliers wrought from it, pictures framed in exquisite carved work of it; tables elegantly inwrought and chairs curiously fashioned of it; statuettes carved from it, coats-of-arms inlaid in amber, elegant vases and artistic carvings and decorations all of the same material, — a most remarkable display. The amber was a present to Catherine, from Frederick the Great.

Another elegant apartment, called the lapis-lazuli room, was inlaid with elegant specimens of that stone, and had a floor of ebony inlaid with flowers of mother-of-pearl, giving a gorgeous effect to the apartment.

In other apartments the walls were completely sheathed in rich silks instead of paper hangings or wood-work. One bedroom had hangings of blue silk, another those of a delicate rose tint with furniture and upholstery of some pleasing contrast, producing an extremely beautiful and luxurious effect.

Ingenuity seems to have been exhausted in prodigal expenditure to produce wonderful effects in these palaces; another room, called the Chinese room, contained some of the richest and rarest specimens of Chinese work I ever looked upon — beautiful vases, silks, rich hangings, brilliant embroideries in silk, jade vases, ornaments, and everything beautifully disposed in ravishing profusion and excellent taste. The bedroom of the Empress Catherine II. was an apartment with porcelain-decorated walls and pillars of rich purple glass.

Then there were the grand banqueting-rooms, which seemed to be almost sheathed in gold, the grand ballrooms elegantly ornamented, and one large room fitted up as a gymnasium, with the usual apparatus, and in addition a toboggan-slide of broad, perfectly polished planks, the toboggan used being a small rug or carpet, and, we being the only visitors present, the slide was then and there satisfactorily tested. The guide who went about with our guide and ourselves was evidently a substitute for the regular officer, who probably thought that an expert like our well known guide only needed a man with him for form's sake, and so pocketed a douceur and deputed a fellow good-naturedly full of vodki to accompany us, who permitted us to do pretty much as we chose, even to handling the personal effects of Alexander I., that remain in his private apartments as he left them; the trying-on of the former emperor's hat and gloves by the author he considered to be more of a joke than an extraordinary liberty.

The Alexander Palace, near at hand, is a tame affair after this one, and contained nothing that specially impressed itself upon my memory, except a series of small models, either of papier-mâché or plaster, of each of the different cavalry regiments of the empire, beautifully done; the uniforms and accoutrements all being correct reproductions of those in use in each of the different bodies of troops, forming a fine military collection. Each figure is about twenty inches in height, and they are kept in glass cases.

CHAPTER XII.

THE journey from St. Petersburg to Moscow occupies from fourteen to fifteen hours. We left at 8.30 P.M., and arrived at Moscow at a few minutes past 11 A.M. the next day — the distance between the two points being four hundred miles. The sleeping-cars were exceedingly comfortable, and similar to those between the frontier and St. Petersburg, and in no way inferior to the best in the United States.

There is but little to interest one on the route, or that portion of it we saw during the few hours of daylight before arrival at Moscow, whose curious-looking spires and bell-shaped cupolas, as we approached it, gave the impression of a city of the East.

Emerging from our comfortable railway carriage, we were soon mounted in a two-horse drosky and whirling away for our hotel. But not through such broad, elegant streets as in St. Petersburg, though the newer part of the city has some fine broad avenues. There was a more semi-Asiatic appearance to things here: curious and grotesque-looking spires; peasants with matted hair and unkempt beards, and who were clad in sheepskins that looked as though they had been owned by several generations, were among the crowds in the street; the Greek-letter-looking signs seemed more undecipherable, the droskies smaller and more dirty, and the vodki shops more frequent; Tartar laborers were more plentiful, and the Asiatic type of face was oftener met, and there seems to be a greater quantity of poorly dressed people in the streets than in St. Petersburg.

Moscow is a manufacturing city; it contains nine hundred manufactories, of various kinds, including many for weaving silk, and employing about one hundred thousand persons. In the whole province of Moscow there are 2506 factories, employing nearly one hundred and ninety thousand work-people, nearly five times as many factories and operatives as are found in St. Petersburg and its environs. Moscow, in fact, is one of the great workshops of Russia. The principal portion of goods manufactured here, I was told, was exported to Central Asia, Asia Minor, and South-eastern Europe.

The cotton industry in Russia has reached great proportions. There are now over one thousand mills and factories turning out cotton fabrics of different kinds, valued at one hundred and fifty million dollars per annum, and giving employment to over two hundred thousand hands. Cotton is raised in Turkestan, Central Asia, and the Caucasus, but, instead of being encouraged and developed, this important industry is neglected. Russia pays annually for imported cotton (mostly from the United States) about seventy-five million roubles in gold, which surpasses three times the annual yield of gold in that country. The parties interested in the cotton industry suggest to the Russian government that it should assist them in developing the cotton plantations in the Merv oasis, the Caucasus, and Turkestan by advancing them sufficient funds. They say that on five hundred thousand acres of choice land they will raise all the cotton Russia will need for her mills. It is improbable, however, that the Russian government will venture in this new business, after so many signal failures.

Two great businesses of national importance, the building of railways and the redemption of land from the former serf-owners, says a recent writer, will particularly drain the imperial treasury for many years. For the former item it has spent since 1848 the enormous sum of 1,440,000,000 roubles ($720,000,000). Finding that the official running of railways did not pay, the government has leased most of its railroads to private companies. Up to this date the government used to guarantee a certain dividend on railroad shares, thus paying to the shareholders about ten million dollars per annum. The railroad companies never pay in full their annual debt to the government, their arrears usually amounting to fifteen million dollars. Up to February 1, 1887, the government had spent for redemption of land for the former serfs $454,000,000, which sum cannot be returned to the treasury for many years to come. As the Russian government does not conduct its finances on business principles, its credit is very poor, be it peace or war. The imperial legal tender — the paper rouble — is now worth only a half of its face value in gold or silver. Though the government pays annually about eighteen million dollars on account of the decline of that paper rouble, yet it is very slow in redeeming it.

The Russian minister of finance, in presenting the state budget for 1887, estimated a deficit of about fifty million dollars, and statistics show that the deficit for the last five years has ranged from twenty-five to fifty millions.

Determined efforts are being made, however, to better the financial condition of affairs. In response to a petition of merchants and statesmen, the czar appointed (1887) a new minister of finance, one Yshonogradsy, who was formerly a professor of mechanics and a railroad-builder, and other changes were made, so that some new system of political economy may be put forward.

The Great Bazaar at Moscow is an exposition of itself, in which each trade has a separate section: jewellers, holy relics and images, bright kerchiefs, fruits, tea-stores, cloth, clothing, boots, shoes, caps, everything in the retail line that one can desire.

That some of the Asiatic customs were prevalent here was evident from the fact that in the Bazaar I noticed clerks in some of the shops figuring out their accounts by the aid of the little wire frame and balls that are in general use among Chinese accountants.

The streets, with very few exceptions, are poorly paved, and you miss the long, stately rows of architectural display that adorn certain quarters of St. Petersburg; for here in Moscow church, hut, and palace are often in close proximity — in fact, everything seems to be more thoroughly mixed in Moscow, and lacking much of the systematic order of the former city.

Here also are the street shrines, little sort of religious shops with the whole side towards the street open and an attendant begging priest or nun or two inside to receive offerings. These shrines are wonderfully numerous, and all receive thorough attention, from the rich man who rolls by in his carriage to the filthiest sheepskin-clad beggar. Not only are the bowing and crossing done by those who pass, but at all hours of the day there are little crowds of men and women at these places bowing and crossing and saying a prayer or two or getting a sip of holy water.

There are, beside the sheepskin-clad peasants that I referred to that one meets, others in the rough blouse that covers a red shirt worn outside the trousers and confined at the waist by a leathern belt, their coarse trousers thrust into a mass of strappings or bandages of bark which serve as boots or shoes. They come into town with loads of wood or other stuff from the country, drawn in carts fashioned in the roughest manner from bent poles and old fragments of wood in the rough, built round four wheels. The wagons used for all purposes that we saw were of a very rude character. Any vehicles corresponding to an American truck, dray, or common express-cart seemed entirely unknown. An American farm-wagon or tip-cart was a far more civilized machine of its kind than any we saw in the streets of Moscow or Petersburg.

We observed that the Russian draught-horses had no traces, but the shafts of the vehicle were attached to their collars. This explains the use of the picturesque, but heavy, high wooden yoke which is worn by these horses in Russia; it holds the shafts a few inches away from the animal, so that he is not shaken by every jolt of the vehicle.

The troïka or Russian travelling-carriage drawn by three horses abreast was familiar to us in school days from the woodcut in our school geographies of one containing two fur-clad individuals with a driver in front of them urging his horses to full speed, and under which appeared the word "Russia." It also appears in some of Schreyer's snow-storm pictures and in the paintings of other artists, so that we imagined the troïka to be a carriage quite in common use. As far as the cities of Petersburg and Moscow are concerned, however, this is not the case, for we saw none in Moscow and but two in St. Petersburg, and those were the private turnouts of wealthy men.

The shock heads of matted hair and full, unkempt beards (growing up to the very eyes) of the peasants, combined with their low foreheads and often brutish countenances, gave some of them the appearance of huge Skye terriers rather than human beings. In cheap bazaars and at crowded church services the sheepskin-clad individuals should be given a wide berth by the tourist, as close contact is by no means pleasant.

The monks here, as in Petersburg, wear long, black robes and tall, cylinder-shaped, black, rimless hats, and from the front of some of the hats fell a veil, partly covering the face. There are two hundred convents and 484 monasteries in Russia, and recent statistics set the number of monks at nearly six thousand and the nuns seven thousand. Until a monk is thirty years of age he is considered a novice, and no woman can become bound to monastic life till she is fifty; at any time before reaching that age she is at liberty to leave the nunnery and marry. There are now attached to the monasteries 4133 lay brethren or novices, and to the convents 14,200 lay sisters.

The singing at the great monastic churches, as I have before remarked, is magnificent, and entirely without musical accompaniment. One of the most remarkable hymns, I was informed, was called the "Thrice Holy," on account of the word "holy" being thrice repeated in its performance.

This and other portions of the service are not in the Russian tongue, but in old Slavonic, as unintelligible to most of the worshippers as the Latin chants and service in the Roman Catholic Church.

It never happened to be my fortune to hear a sermon preached in a Russian church; but an English writer speaks of them as being peculiarly adapted to the Russian mind, because they appeal to the feelings rather than the intellect.

The peculiar bulb-shaped domes of the churches continually suggested to me the mosques of an Eastern city, heightened as they were in barbaric appearance by being painted green, or glittering with copper or gilding.

The story of Bonaparte's invasion of Russia, the conflagration of Moscow, his disastrous retreat therefrom, and the annihilation of his spendid army has done more to excite a desire to see that city, among English-speaking people, than anything else in its history. I remember, years ago, an exhibition that was thought to be quite a wonderful affair, called "The Conflagration of Moscow," which was exhibited in all the principal cities of America, in conjunction with that wonderful piece of deception known as Maelzel's Automaton Chess-Player. This panoramic exhibition was a most effective affair in its way ; on the curtain rising, the city by moonlight was revealed, with its bulb-like towers and domes glittering in the moon's rays. The Kremlin occupied the foreground, and turrets, spires, and bridges were seen in the distance. Soon, afar off, were heard the drums of the approaching French troops, and at the same time a distant flame lighted up a small space of sky with its rays, and the great bells began to boom the alarm.

The fire spread and clouds of smoke rolled upwards; meantime, the people could be seen flying with their household goods ; the glare of the increasing conflagration now lighted up the whole scene. The city, with its spires, pinnacles, bridges, walls, and the Kremlin were now visible ; so were little figures of incendiaries, with torches busy with the work of destruction. The peal of the fire-bells was incessant, the great clouds of smoke rolled skyward, and walls of houses and steeples crashed down amid myriads of sparks. Now the drum of the troops and the military bands were heard distinctly, and we saw them in the panoramic representation, crossing the bridges and entering the city; the brass cannon glittered in the fire-light, and the shining bayonets of the foot-soldiers were seen as they marched in solid columns.

At the very height of the conflagration, according to the printed programme, "the Kremlin is blown up, with a terrific explosion, by the mines of gunpowder placed beneath it by the Russians." And so concluded a very effective panoramic exhibition, which, together with the story of Napoleon's campaign, always made me long to see Russia's ancient capital, whose inhabitants sacrificed it rather than yield to the invader. I found it well worth the brief visit made it, and in many respects a more thoroughly Russian city than St. Petersburg. It is, as is well known, a much older one, and is generally considered a very good specimen of the old Russian cities.

Moscow is celebrated for its churches, of which there are said to be nearly four hundred. It has been the scene of the coronations of the czars and of the cruelties of Ivan the Terrible, the reading of which makes one inclined to wish, if he does not believe there is a state of future punishment, that a hell might have been invented for the especial torture of that human fiend.

Moscow is named after the river Moskva. It seems to be a vast circle in form, with the triangular fortress of the Kremlin in the centre. Our headquarters were the Hotel Dusaux, a well kept, large hotel, with fine, clean apartments, excellent cuisine, and moderate rates of charge, entirely at variance with English accounts, which had led us to believe that the accommodations were inferior and charges high. Neither the hotel in Moscow nor that in St. Petersburg was inferior to the Grand or Metropole in London, as regards apartments, cuisine, and attendance.

I could hardly realize being in the old Russian capital, until, looking out of the windows, we saw the walls of the Kremlin, with its quaint towers, and heard the rattle of droskies, saw the Russian drivers in their curious costumes driving them, the curious signs, and the rough-looking people passing and repassing.

But our guide has the team of black stallions ready at the door, and we start for our first view of the sights of the city.

The Kremlin!

This is the first feature of Moscow that rises in your imagination when you read or speak of the city before you visit it, the one sight of all others you desire to see and the most interesting one that you do see after arrival in this ancient and sacred city of the empire.

"Kremlin" really means fortress or citadel, and comes from a Tartar word having that signification. It is really a great enclosure, two miles in circuit, which is crowded with churches, palaces, arsenals, watch-towers, and steeples of every conceivable design. The best collective view of it is had from the river-side, and within its walls are the most interesting historical sights in Moscow. It is looked upon by the Russians with something of the veneration with which the English regard the Tower of London, and its history, although not beginning so early, goes back to 1367, since when down to 1812 it went through various vicissitudes and was largely added to and improved. Napoleon, on leaving after his invasion, made unsuccessful attempts to destroy it, but it still stands a proud and central monument of Holy Moscow.

There are five great gates of entrance to the Kremlin, and the one that we first entered was that we had heard so much of, called "The Redeemer's Gate," from its having a picture of our Saviour suspended over the archway, which, it is said, has been there since the foundation of the city, and which is believed to have such miraculous power that in ancient times the Tartar hordes were never able to pass it, nor could in latter days the powder-mines of the French army destroy it.

The archway is beneath a magnificent square tower, surmounted by various small spires and a lofty steeple. The whole Kremlin seems to be girdled with odd-looking towers of ancient construction, some dating back to 1485.

We were warned by the guide to uncover our heads as we passed through the archway of the Redeemer Gate and beneath the picture, as every one, even the emperor himself, is expected to do so, and does, so that even American travellers are not an exception to this rule. Before ascending the tower of Ivan, we halted to look at the great bell that stands on a little raised brick platform at its base. This big bell is twenty-six feet high, sixty-seven feet in circumference, and two feet in thickness; a great piece seven feet high, which is broken out of its side, stands near it.

The weight of this metallic giant is four hundred and forty-four thousand pounds, and as one gazes upon its vast bulk the question arises how it could be raised to the proper home of a bell, a steeple, and what force beside steam-power could ring it effectually, and how it would sound when it was rung.

Speaking of bells, the tower of Ivan the Great is a

veritable tower of bells, for we found four or five stories, one above another, as we ascended, filled with bells, of various descriptions and dimensions, sizes and tones, which we amused ourselves by tapping with our knuckles and pocket-knives in an endeavor to bring out some indication of musical tones, for which they are celebrated.

In one tier we saw two small bells entirely of silver and of exquisite tone; in another the monster of the collection, weighing sixty-four tons, a huge and ponderous affair, but not one-half the weight of the broken monster we had inspected outside the tower.

This tower is the loftiest in the city, and is built in five different stories, the last cylindrical and surmounted by the bulb, Tartar-looking cupola so common here, but which has such a foreign, Asiatic look to American eyes. The bells, which are thirty-four in number, are suspended in the three lower stories.

The dome is brightly gilded and glitters in the sunlight, and from its height attracts attention from whatever point one views the city, for the top of the great cross above our heads is 325 feet above the pavement. A fine view of the city and surrounding country was had after our tiresome climb, showing us the Moskva River at our feet, the closely crowded buildings inside the Kremlin, the circle after circle of the city's structures, bounded by ramparts, the innumerable towers and steeples golden, green, silver, red, and white, and beyond all the green fields and foliage of the country. It is a striking and indescribable panoramic view, and unlike any other I have seen in Europe.

Riding past the arsenal in the Kremlin, we saw displayed the cannon taken from and abandoned by Napoleon during his disastrous retreat from Moscow.

They are 365 in number, and ranged along on raised platforms outside the walls of the building; some of these were left in the city, and others captured by the Russians and Cossacks hundreds of miles away, as they hung upon the flanks of the retreating army, which was harassed by cold and hunger and the fierce onslaught of its incensed adversaries.

Besides these French cannon there are numerous others, that have been captured from Austria, Sweden, Italy, and Spain, the entire lot forming a big park of about nine hundred pieces of artillery. There was also a huge Russian cannon standing not far from the tower we had just left, its bore big as a hogshead, and the piece weighing forty tons; it was cast in 1586 and is called the Czar cannon, and would doubtless do more damage to those operating it than to those against whom it was directed. The arsenal is said to contain arms sufficient to equip one hundred and fifty thousand men.

A wonderful building of its kind in Moscow is a huge structure known as the Riding-School and designed for the use of drilling cavalry or infantry in severe weather. The vast extent of roofing is unsupported by pillar of any kind, affording a space of one hundred and sixty feet in width by nearly six hundred in length, in which, it is said, two entire regiments of cavalry can go through with their evolutions. The heating apparatus consists of huge earthen stoves, and the sides of the walls are decorated with trophies of arms. A peculiar arrangement of trusses and stays supports the vast roof; but, as the whole was undergoing repairs at the time of our visit, we were not permitted to examine its peculiar structure. It is undoubtedly the largest riding-school in the world.

The Cathedral of the Assumption, situated within

the walls of the Kremlin, is another one of those wonderful Russian churches teeming with wealth, and which one can get but an imperfect idea of in the hour or two occupied by the tourist in inspecting it. This church is interesting as being the one in which the Russian emperors are crowned, and as retaining very nearly its original form. It was built in 1325.

When the French occupied Moscow, this church yielded rich spoil to the soldiers, for they stripped it of over twelve hundred pounds weight of silver and five hundred pounds of gold. Much of the silver was recovered from the plunderers and replaced.

The height of this cathedral is one hundred and twenty-eight feet. It has five magnificent domes, which we stood under and gazed upon the beautiful pillars supporting them, the gilded walls, statues, and frescos on every side forming a grand display of riches and architectural beauty. The screen is rich in the possession of a painting of the Virgin, of course possessed of miraculous powers, and is literally overwhelmed with rich jewels, such as diamonds, sapphires, emeralds, and rubies.

There are nearly two hundred and fifty thousand dollars worth of jewels upon this painting, including a huge emerald worth over forty thousand dollars. The screen is adorned with numerous other paintings of religious subjects and scenes. A great silver shrine stands on the right of the screen, and contains the body of St. Philip, a priest who was bold enough to rebuke that human fiend Ivan the Terrible, and suffered death therefor. Splendid tombs at different corners of the church mark the resting-places of priests or other dignitaries.

Being admitted behind the great altar-screen, we saw

more of the treasures of this wonderful church. Here was a representation of Mt. Sinai, made of solid gold and silver, containing the Host; about twenty pounds of each of the precious metals were used in its construction. Among other rich relics is a huge Bible, so large that it requires the united strength of two men to carry it. This was presented to the church by Peter the Great's mother, and the binding is one mass of precious stones, a perfect mine of them, worth hundreds of thousands of dollars.

The eye grows weary of this profuse and prodigal display of wealth, so that we turn from rich golden cups studded with jewels, magnificent jasper vases, golden crosses sparkling with gems, golden marriage-crowns, and magnificent vestments, to the relics which the church considers of a most sacred character, such as a piece of the true cross, the hand of St. Andrew and head of St. Gregory, a portion of the robe of the Saviour, and others that I cannot recall, all of which were kindly and reverently displayed to us by an attendant priest or sacristan, who had been encouraged by a handsome fee and was courteous and deferential to his curious American visitors.

Within the nave of the church was the ancient throne of the czars, also that of the patriarch of the church, and a throne for the empress. The walls were lined with paintings — in fact, a perfect mass of gilded pictures.

Close by the cathedral we had just visited was another, that of the Archangel Michael, a square, white-looking building, with five gilded domes shining above it. This church is remarkable for containing the tombs of Russian sovereigns previous to Peter the Great; there are forty-five of these tombs in the church, each covered with a pall, and above them are painted pictures of the departed, clad in long white robes.

Next to the altar, probably from the fact of his being the greatest sinner known in Russian royal history, is the tomb of John the Terrible, and behind the altar-screen you are shown a cross that once belonged to him, covered with huge pearls, with an enormous emerald in the middle of it.

The Treasury here is, as its name indicates, a depository of rich and valuable objects. Like many other places of interest, I can give but the merest sketch of the contents of this wonderful collection. To give a complete account would require repeated lengthy visits, and space that would fill a volume. Rich plate, precious stones, gold and silver vessels and vases, trophies of arms, specimens of barbaric splendor and costly manufacture, which Russia has been collecting for years from India, Persia, Turkey, and Greece, are here in profusion, and indicate the prodigal magnificence of the Russian court.

Gifts, trophies, and relics are on every side of the bewildered visitor. One room is full of Russian and Circassian armor of every description, elegantly fashioned and inwrought with gold; in another, in which were trophies captured by the Russian troops on different occasions, was the sword of Charles XII., the Lion of Sweden; a third contained a complete assortment of Russian fire-arms, from the rude inventions of the fifteeth century down to the rifles used at the present time — a most interesting collection of arms; here also were groups of military standards, all historical, having been carried during different wars. One was that used by John the Terrible in 1552.

Time permitted only a glance at a room full of portraits of the Romanoff family, and another of relics relating to the Russian royal family. Were Americans generally as familiar with the history of Russian sovereigns as they are with that of English and French, I doubt not this would be a most interesting portion of the collection. As for us, we could only ask our guide to jot down, in note-book or memory, the names of such as by their peculiar appearance attracted our attention.

We visited a room called the Wardrobe, containing crowns upon pedestals standing before empty thrones of departed monarchs. These crowns and thrones are weighty with rubies, sapphires, and emeralds, some of them big as walnuts or horse-chestnuts. One of these crowns was conspicuous even among this collection of prodigal wealth. It was a tall, mitre-shaped affair surmounted by a big ruby, from which rose a splendid diamond cross; the crown itself contained no less than nine hundred sparkling diamonds: this valuable headpiece was that of John, the brother of Peter I. The crown of another Russian emperor, whose name I understood to be Michael, had a huge emerald upon the top of it and about two hundred other precious stones about it. An orb used at coronations was profusely ornamented with diamonds and eight of the biggest sapphires I ever saw.

It was hard to believe that the gems ornamenting these crowns could be real, so large was there size and so profusely were they used. But prodigality outdid itself in the wonderful crown made by order of Peter the Great for the Empress Catherine I. Just think of the weight and value of this affair, which contains, besides other costly stones, two thousand five hundred and thirty diamonds! Other crowns, with the same profuse display of pearls, diamonds, turquoises, amethysts, and elegant enamel-work, seemed but repetitions of lapidaries' efforts to produce novel specimens of their work.

Among these were two famous thrones, one the royal throne of Poland, taken in 1833 from Warsaw, and an ivory throne that was brought from Constantinople, which was curiously carved with figures representing some allegory or fable. But a throne that carries out one's youthful ideas of what a throne should be, a sort of Arabian-Nights-entertainment or fairy-legend affair, is one that was brought from Persia in 1660, which is studded all over with a wealth of precious stones, as though it had been out in a hard shower of turquoises, sapphires, diamonds, and rubies; — of these there are over one thousand two hundred rubies and 875 diamonds.

Here also are an orb, crown, and collar sent to Vladimir, Grand-Duke of Kief, by the Emperors Basilius and Constantine, from Greece — one perfect blaze of diamonds and rubies. The orb has 58 diamonds, 89 rubies, 23 sapphires, 50 emeralds, and 37 pearls.

Such profuse and lavish display of costly gems and precious metals as one sees in these Russian treasuries, churches, and palaces has the effect of belittling their value in one's mind; and the practical financier cannot help estimating how much of the empire's national debt they would extinguish if disposed of at present market-value, or how much good this dead capital might do in advancing the cause of education among the densely ignorant peasantry of the country.

In this room were various articles of wearing-apparel of different noted members of the royal family, as well as the magnificent coronation-robes of others: the military dress of Peter II., the books of Peter I. and Paul I., the English Order of the Garter sent by Queen Elizabeth to John the Terrible; the coronation-robes of Catherine I. and Catherine II., and those of Alexander I., Paul, Nicholas I., and others, including those of the present emperor and empress. The throne of Boris Godunof was another gorgeous affair, covered all over with rubies, pearls, and turquoises.

Then we were shown a curious double-seated throne, said to have been made for Peter I. and his brother John, with a concealed recess behind it, which was contrived for John's sister Sophia to prompt him on occasions. She was literally "the power behind the throne," and perhaps this may be the origin of that expression.

From this hall of wealth and riches we passed into another scarcely less wonderful, for it was one that reminded us more than anything else of a grand exhibition of the silver-workers of the world. It was a collection, apparently, of every known domestic utensil, fashioned from the precious metal. Not only those of the present day, but rare and curious antiques, some of priceless value and by the best artificers of all nations. One great pitcher, beautifully wrought, weighed twenty pounds; a beautiful antique cup bore an inscription of the twelfth century. Then there were gifts innumerable from various royal personages to the czar; salvers with elegant hunting-scenes carved on them; pitchers with handles wrought into flowers, birds, or animals; jugs surmounted by knights in armor, and a bewildering museum of elegant and artistic models in silver-work.

It would be like a descriptive catalogue to enumerate the curious objects of lesser note in the other rooms of the Treasury, but I will mention the model of a new palace which that extravagant sovereign Catherine II. planned, which would have been a quarter of a mile long when completed, but, as she died soon after the corner-stone was laid, the ambitious and costly project was abandoned.

The museum of carriages here in the Treasury, although not so extensive a collection as that at St. Petersburg, is still an interesting one. Conspicuous is one of those huge affairs that one sees pictures of in old English story-books or illustrations of Queen Elizabeth's time, and is in fact a specimen of the carriage-building of that age, as the vehicle was presented by Queen Bess to the Czar Boris Godunof. It is elegantly gotten up, and its panels are adorned with paintings of battle-scenes. Then there is a little carriage used by one of the emperors when a child; another, a huge affair, belonging to the Empress Elizabeth, which could be used as a dining-room for herself and twelve of her suite. The panels of this are also beautifully painted. We regarded with interest two of Napoleon's camp-bedsteads, captured from him during his Russian campaign.

Another depository of richness, of a somewhat different description, was the Patriarch's Sacristy. This place contains many very curious articles connected with the history of the Greek Church, and some of great antiquity. Here is kept a wonderful collection of silver vessels, massive in size and weight, used in the preparation of a sacred mixture for baptismal and anointing purposes. According to the rule of the church, every true Russian should be baptized with the sacred oil, or *mir*, so called.

The original of this sacred mixture was, it is said,

sent from Constantinople to Russia on its being converted to Christianity, and we were shown the beautiful vase said to contain the precious liquid. A few drops of this are taken each year to mix with the huge quantity of *mir* prepared by the priests, with much ceremony, to be distributed to churches in different parts of the empire. The ingredients composing the sacred mixture are over thirty in number, including essential oils, gums, perfumes, herbs, spices, etc., which are boiled together with great care in three huge silver kettles, one a veritable caldron presented by Catherine II. After boiling and cooling, the few drops of original sacred oil are dropped in, which are supposed to pervade and sanctify the whole. It is then turned off into sixteen or eighteen great silver jars and ready for distribution as above mentioned. The ceremony of preparing this mixture occurs once in every three years, and is performed during Lent, by the highest officials of the church.

The vases, basins, ladles, great caldrons and strainers used for this purpose, which were shown to us, were all of sterling silver, and their value may be estimated from the fact that their weight, as our guide told us, was about fourteen hundred pounds, avoirdupois. The place was in care of a venerable and noble-looking Russian priest, of the most courteous and dignified bearing, and who, strange to relate, refuses to receive any fee from visitors. Our guide was careful to advise us, however, that he would appreciate highly a ceremonious and deferential leave-taking, as he was a man of noble family. Thereupon, after having inspected the treasures of which he was the guardian, on our way out, as we were about to pass him, we halted and made a profound obeisance. This he returned, rising from his seat, bowing in deferential style, and bidding us adieu with a graceful wave of the hand.

This house of the Holy Synod, as it is called, contains the holy robes, ornaments, church-vessels, etc., of the various patriarchs of the church, some of which were brought here from Constantinople. The patriarchs of the church were invested with their holy robes at consecration, and one of the oldest of these, which was shown to us, was one worn in the year 1308. The most remarkable one of this collection, which, despite its richness, reminds one of the wardrobe of the Grand Opera, is an elaborate one presented by that inhuman monster, John the Terrible, to the patriarch of his time. Royal murderers and tyrants like him seem to have believed they could purchase forgiveness for their wickedness and crimes by gifts to the church, seeking to ease their consciences in this manner, often by wealth wrung from their subjects by cruel oppression. This robe is of rich crimson velvet and thickly covered with pearls, gold plates, diamonds, rubies, and emeralds — so thickly covered that it weighs fifty-four pounds. A description of the numerous others would be, as the lawyers say, only "cumulative evidence" of velvet dresses lavishly ornamented with jewelry.

The mitres, like the crowns I have referred to, are simply wonderful specimens of jewelry-work. The largest one weighs nearly six pounds, and is encrusted with big diamonds, rubies, emeralds, and pearls. Among the rarest articles in this collection that I recall were some huge gems beautifully carved, and worn in chains by the priests.

Only think of such jewels strung on a chain for a priest's necklace as two great sardonyxes, $3\frac{3}{4}$ inches long and $2\frac{1}{2}$ inches wide, beautifully carved and engraved with holy scenes and religious subjects! A great onyx bore upon it a fine carving representing the Crucifixion, and at the back of another is shown a fragment said to be of the robe of our Saviour, and a piece of stone from Calvary! Richly decorative croziers, vases, goblets, and dishes, of solid gold and silver, and other ecclesiastical treasures, also are kept here.

CHAPTER XIII.

ONE of the very oldest churches in the Kremlin, and, in fact, in Moscow, is that known as "The Church in the Wood," because when it was built it was literally in the woods, though now close to the palace. It is a curious little building to visit, and in striking contrast to its more magnificent neighbors, with its rude frescos upon its walls and narrow passages. It was used as a nunnery in the fifteenth century, and as a forage-stable by Napoleon in 1812.

Near the Redeemer's Gate, just outside the walls of the Kremlin, is the church known as St. Basil the Beautiful. It is a curious conglomeration of Eastern architecture, a heterogeneous collection of domes, spires, and steeples. There is a central octagon spire surrounded by eight smaller ones with the Tartar or bulb-shaped cupolas. Then there is an indescribable mixture of pinnacles, peaks, and domes springing out in every direction, and the whole building is richly gilded, fluted, carved, and ornamented till it shines like a Chinese pagoda and reminds one of such a temple on a large scale as Barnum, the American showman, might put up. It certainly is the most curious exhibition, as a specimen of indescribable architecture, I ever saw. It might be called Tartar architecture from the general appearance.

I counted twelve domes, every one of which was of different design, and many of these presented different colors and were ornamented in a different manner.

These domes and others stand over the chapels of different saints within the building, which you reach by passing through narrow passages between the walls, thick enough for a fortress and decorated with frescos representing old tapestry. There were a great number of small chapels in this church, some rich with votive offerings, and we saw nothing worthy of note except several heavy iron chains that St. Basil was said to have worn as necklaces and sashes by way of penance and mortification during his lifetime, and which are now hung up above his tomb.

The great cathedral of St. Saviour here is evidently designed to rival St. Isaac's of Petersburg; it is a magnificent structure, grand beyond description, and one which meets your eye from every prominent point of view in the city. Its form is that of a Greek cross, and it has the usual magnificent domes of the Russian churches; the great central dome is three hundred feet in circumference, and there are four smaller ones.

These five great cupolas, we were told, were of copper, and in gilding them over nine hundred pounds of pure gold were required. Everything about the building, within and without, is on a scale of grand proportions and the most prodigal splendor. Its appearance is one mass of shining white marble, with the gorgeous cupolas rising above, and its great cross thirty feet high flashing against the sky, three hundred and forty feet above the ground, is stupendous and overwhelming.

This church was erected as a memorial temple of Napoleon's retreat from Moscow, and it is but quite recently that it has been completed. Its expense must of course have been millions, inasmuch as the site alone cost nearly a million of dollars before the foundations were laid, and the doors alone of the edifice, now that it is completed, cost over three hundred thousand dollars. It stands upon a beautiful natural slope overlooking one of the principal bridges, and has fine grounds or gardens about it, filled with trees, plants, and flowers. The exterior is richly decorated with carved figures in alto-relievo. I omitted to mention that the church has what no Russian church would be complete without, a splendid chime of bells. The monarch of the group is a deep-toned giant of twenty-six tons weight.

Within, all is one gorgeous display of magnificently wrought marble, jasper, and porphyry. The sides are of different kinds of marble, beautifully polished; great columns of jasper and rhodonite support the roof. The inside of the dome is richly frescoed with scenes from the life of Christ, and the screen one mass of elegant wrought work and gilding. All along one side of the church are scenes from the War of 1812, painted by Russian artists. The view looking up as one stands beneath the great dome is superb.

The church, as stated, having been finished but a few years, was at the time of our visit in its newest gloss as regards richness of gilding, freshness of frescos, and sheen of polished marbles.

The height from floor to ceiling, within, is 230 feet, and the floor, which is entirely of marble, is 225 feet square, and cost a million and a half dollars. You feel dwarfed amid such grand proportions, for the building will hold over ten thousand people, and your guide, knowing the American propensity to ask the cost of things, launches out the big figures of some of the items, like 375,000 roubles, or over one hundred and thirty thousand dollars, for six hundred and forty great candelabra that stand in one row, and which, when filled with lighted wax candles, must produce a superb effect. There are over twelve hundred of these candelabra in all, costing about two hundred thousand dollars.

Behind the screen, in the Sanctum Sanctorum of the patriarch, were some very fine modern paintings of scriptural subjects, besides relics and rich vessels belonging to the church, which we were desirous of seeing, but an incorruptible guardian stood at the entrance. Our guide, however, was equal to the occasion. He bade us stand quietly while he went to interview the principal priest, a tall, venerable man, who stood not far from us, engaged in conversation with two other priests or monks.

As soon as the latter left the priest, our guide approached with profound obeisance, which was returned, took him by the hand, said a few sentences to the reverend father, who turned towards where we were standing with a grave bow of the head. We returned the salutation with hand on heart, after the manner of the tragedian called before the curtain at the end of a successful performance.

This was followed by an imperative wave of the hand by the priest to the official on duty at the entrance of the sanctuary, which had a magical effect, changing him from the inflexible guardian to the most deferential of servitors as he conducted us within the sacred limits, where were some superb large paintings by native artists, one (if memory serves me) from the pencil of the artist who painted the "Russian Wedding," which has excited so much attention in America. The light is so managed, by windows above, as to give a wonderfully fine effect to these paintings.

The spacious interior of this church is less floridly

decorated than the older Russian churches, but the marbles and stone-work are equally elegant and expensive. The gilding upon the five domes cost an amount equal to seven hundred and fifty thousand dollars of our money.

This magnificent temple we rode around again after leaving it, to take in its grand extent and beautiful proportions. Its foundation is entirely of granite brought from the quarries of Finland, and the structure covers an area of over seventy-three thousand feet, and is surrounded by grounds beautifully laid out and bright with many-colored flowers at the time of our visit. I am in doubt as to whether this or St. Isaac's is the most imposing structure. The former is grand and imposing, but the prevailing characteristic of St. Saviour's is its beauty, and the visitor lingers from point to point, loath to leave so luxurious a treat of exquisite finish and proportions.

Upon reëntering our carriage, after visiting this church, I inquired of the guide what words he used with such magical effect upon the priest by whose favor we received such attention.

"I mentioned to him," said he, "that it was a pity that the American consul and his secretary should be debarred from visiting all parts of this church, of which they had heard so much and travelled so far to see."

"American consul! Why, I hold no such office!"

"I am aware of it, and did not say that you did. Nevertheless, that reference gained you the bow that you were thoughtful enough to return."

"Indeed!"

"Yes. I then intimated that you desired me to make a small offering to the church, which was done when I shook hands with him and conveyed three roubles to his palm."

"That accounted for the withdrawal and courtesy of the guard?"

"Yes, that and another rouble to the aforesaid guard; roubles purchase many privileges in Russia."

One of the most wonderful institutions in Moscow is the foundling hospital. This is an enormous building, not far from the Kremlin. Some idea of its size may be had from the fact that it has 2228 windows and that it receives over fifteen thousand children annually. While we sat in the office of reception, three came in within half an hour. No questions are asked, except if the child has been baptized and what are its name and age; these are at once entered upon a book and ticket, the boys' on a ticket of one color and girls' upon a ticket of another color. Neither are these children deposited surreptitiously at the door, but brought in by relatives and even their own mothers. After being properly registered by three young women (themselves former foundlings), the infant has a number placed around its neck, corresponding to a number given to the person bringing it to the institution; it is then taken into another room, where it is received by trained nurses, and then given in charge of one of the numerous nurses in attendance, who washes it and dresses it. Soon after it is subjected to a thorough medical examination to see if it is suffering from any disease, and if found to be is sent at once to a ward of the hospital devoted to such, where it has the best of medical care and attention. Infants remain in the institution one month, during which time they are vaccinated, and then, if found in healthy condition, they are sent with their nurse to the village to which the latter belongs, she receiving a sum equal to about a dollar and a quarter per month for care of the infant until it becomes of age, and under the supervision of the doctor of the district, who is accountable to the government authorities.

Of course, a very large proportion of these children are of illegitimate birth, but the mothers contrive (if they desire it) to keep track of their offspring by means of the ticket given them, and also, as many of them do, by tattooing a small mark upon the arm or some portion of the body. Furthermore, as nurses are in constant demand, mothers do not hesitate to apply for positions in that capacity, and seek with good success to obtain their own children. So it would appear that the mother of an illegitimate child receives a premium of a dollar and a quarter per week for its support. The mother may claim the child at any time before it is ten years of age "by proving property and (without) paying charges."

The boys, when old enough, are liable to military service; some are taught trades at an industrial school in Moscow, others become agricultural laborers. The girls are trained in various occupations, including domestic service; many of them are taken back to the hospital and taught to be trained nurses, and here let me say a more perfect system of faithful, thorough, and careful treatment does not seem possible than that which we saw in passing through the wards of this vast hospital.

Every part of it is scrupulously neat and under the best of medical and domestic management, even to the minutest details. The infants are bathed in conveniently shaped flannel-lined tubs, dressed upon pillows made for the purpose, and handled with the utmost care and dexterity by the nurses, who seem to be wonderful adepts at their work. The corps of physicians and surgeons is large, and the most rigid skill is exercised not only in the care of the infants, but as regards the food and comfort of the wet-nurses.

It is something of a sight one sees in going into this great community of twelve or fifteen hundred babies and nearly a thousand wet-nurses. In one of the great wards it was visiting day, and there were many young mothers in to see and some to take farewell of their offspring, giving instructions to the nurses to whom they had been assigned, or covertly taking a farewell kiss and tearful adieu of some little slumberer in its white cot. Some of these were by no means from the poorest walks of life. Many of the latter contrive to get employment and assignment to their own children.

From the wards where the new-comers were washed, inspected, and fed on first arrival, we passed through room after room of others who were passing their month of probation in the institution; and the moderate amount of outcry, the comfort and cleanliness of cots and nurses and all the surroundings attested the degree of perfection to which the management of the establishment and the care of the infants have been carried.

The sick-wards are characterized by the same care, and have nurses who have been trained in the treatment of different complaints, even to those of many poor little creatures whose hours of life were already numbered. Not only this, but one department was devoted to the care of children of premature birth. These little creatures are placed in large, egg-shaped, copper cradles, lined with soft flannels, the bottom and sides of the cradle being filled with hot water, kept at carefully regulated temperature, and provided with a glazed top affording a view of the occupant who is undergoing this process of bringing forward.

The bodies of such as die during the month are subjected to post-mortem examination, and a full report made by the examining surgeons as to the cause of death, and other facts resulting from the examination, so that it will be seen the hospital affords to the student also one of the best and most practical medical schools for the study of the diseases of children. After a walk through the different wards of the vast building, we next visited its refectories for nurses, the laundries, bakery, kitchen, etc.

In a room off the bakery were great frames or open shelves where hundreds and hundreds of loaves of bread were stored; the coarse brown bread of the country for ordinary attendants, and more nutritious loaves for the wet-nurses. The latter were also allowed a certain amount of a sort of beer, a mild and cheap Russian concoction said to contain many nutritive qualities.

The laundries, bakeries, and cooking arrangements seemed to be of the most approved description, and on the extensive scale required for this institution, which must employ some thousands within its walls. The women serving as nurses get about a dollar and thirty cents per week besides the good fare provided for them by the institution. The yearly grant of the government to it is about one million of dollars. Although this hospital seems to encourage immorality and fraud, yet the Russians tell us that not 5 per cent. of the births of Russia are illegitimate, although statistics also show that in Moscow and St. Petersburg, where these foundling hospitals are located, the percentage runs up to over 25 or 35 per cent. — Moscow taking the lead, and also leading Paris 10 per cent.

The managers of the hospital informed us that a very large proportion of the children brought to the hospital were of legitimate birth, their parents being of the laboring class, and at service at such low wages that they could give neither the time nor the means to bring up their children, and, being assured of better care than they could give, resigned them here, with the hope of claiming them before they reached the age of ten years. Notwithstanding its excellent management, the institution may perhaps in many respects be considered a questionable charity.

The yearly grant to this hospital from the government is nearly a million of dollars. The number of foundlings left annually here has reached the number of 13,865, but it is a question whether any increase of population is effected by these foundling hospitals, for there is said to be great mortality among the children after leaving the hospital, owing to the rigor of the climate and the rough peasant-fare they are obliged to put up with; for the dull, monotonous life of the Russian peasantry must be dreary in the extreme — indeed, far below that of the North American savage as far as liberty, freedom, and exercise are concerned, and the brutish faces of some of them that we saw were below those, in point of intellect, of the Digger Indian of North America.

No visitor to Moscow will think of leaving the city without a ride out to Sparrow Hills, the point where Napoleon Bonaparte obtained his first view of Moscow, when he made that most wonderful crusade of modern times, the invasion of Russia, with his vast and well equipped army — a wonderful achievement by the greatest soldier of the age, followed by his most disastrous of defeats — the complete annihilation of his mighty host.

Moscow, it will be remembered, is a far more ancient city than St. Petersburg. It was founded nearly eight hundred years ago, defended against Tamerlane the Tartar, burned by Tartar invaders, but, rising Phœnix-like from repeated conflagrations, it was recognized as the Muscovite capital in the fourteenth century, and was, and is still, dear to the heart of every true Russian.

The burning of this holy city of Russia is described as the grandest sacrifice ever made by a nation, that, finding it could not be defended from victorious foes, chose to destroy the dearest treasure of the Russian heart, the holiest of her shrines, and the precious memories of centuries, rather than they should be enjoyed by the conquerors.

There are said to be 350 churches in Moscow, or, counting all places of worship, 365 — one for every day in the year; and the city itself seems to be surrounded by two or three grand boulevards or causeways, which are said to mark the site of ancient fortifications against incursions of the Tartars. But Moscow is fast becoming a great centre of manufactures and a commercial and business city, the railway system affording means for reception of material and distribution of products, so that ere long the semi-barbaric architecture and flavor of Eastern life which it now possesses will gradually give way to the advance of European ideas and the pronounced features of modern civilization.

It was over a bridge across the Moskva River, near Sparrow Hills, that one of the main columns of the French army passed on entering the city. The ride to this point is over a very bad road, but, the point once gained, the view is worth seeing. A small hotel is built upon a prominent point here, with a broad covered platform, upon which you may sit and enjoy the fragrant and delicious glass of Russian tea with its floating slice of lemon, and such other light refreshment as you may order, and look down upon the glittering display of spires, domes, steeples, and churches, with their gilded points flashing in the sunshine and their odd and variegated colors seeming like a huge kaleidoscope in the distance.

Near here, on Salutation Hill, Napoleon sat, surrounded by his staff, on the 14th of September, 1812, gazing upon the walls of the distant Kremlin, the glittering spires and gilded domes of the city, while a division of his army in battle array at the foot awaited in vain the advance of the Russian army that he expected would defend their holy city. But none came, and his advanced guard, under Murat, entered the city and took possession of the Kremlin, Napoleon himself following the next day.

No sooner, however, was the conqueror within the ancient palace than the development of Russian tactics began with the conflagration, and, after a stay of a little over a month, Napoleon was compelled to abandon the city and began his disastrous retreat, in which only forty thousand men out of the Grand Army escaped the general wreck.

It is interesting to imaginative minds to stand upon spots like this, so celebrated in history. Here where the great soldier gazed upon the goal of his ambition, or at Waterloo, where lay the Guards whose withering fire hurled back the hitherto invincible Imperial Guard and settled the fate of the modern Cæsar, the mind must be dull indeed not to be stirred by the recollection of the stirring scenes that were there enacted.

On our ride back to Moscow we passed the houses

of the Russian peasants, rough-looking cabins made of peeled logs, somewhat after the style of Western American log cabins. In Russian villages, even of considerable size, all the houses, with the exception of two or three, which are the residences of officials, are poor and wretched-looking affairs, but the church will be found rich, and often blazing with precious metal enough to purchase the whole settlement.

The poorer class of peasants we saw on the road, when returning, were in rough, coarse clothing and sheepskin garments, and at the corner of one house or workshop was a group about to enjoy their evening meal, which appeared to be a round tub of sour beer into which chopped-up bits of cold cabbage and cucumbers had been thrown.

But soon after passing this group we met a sadder sight — a procession of Siberian exiles guarded by mounted Cossack soldiers, on their long march to that region of banishment and captivity. This band was thirty or forty in number, chained together in couples, some wearing chains from the wrists to the ankles; the latter were said to be either thieves or murderers. Behind these prisoners, who were on foot, came six or eight rude carts in which were the wives and children of some of the prisoners, who were permitted to accompany them. According to the laws of the empire, a man exiled to Siberia is legally dead, and his wife may marry again. These gangs of convicts march from eight to twelve miles a day and are served with rations of biscuit and salt beef, and such water as they can get by the way. There is, however, a general feeling of pity felt for them all along the route, and the inhabitants of the villages through which they pass set out bread, cabbage soup, and jugs of beer for them by the roadside, which they are permitted to take as they pass. No one is allowed to approach or speak to them on the march, which is a long and painful one, and the fatigues of which, combined with the sufferings of having often to bivouac in the pine-forests or on the barren steppes with insufficient shelter, cause many to perish on the six or eight weeks' terrible march. The group which passed us had few whose countenances or appearance gave any indications that they were other than degraded specimens of their class.

Later on, when we encountered another group near Nijni Novgorod, there were many of a much better personal appearance that might have been political prisoners, but they were chained together, men and women, with others of the vilest and most brutal physiognomy, and I am told that alleged women conspirators and female thieves and murderers are linked together in the gang, or delicate females who have been accused of promoting treasonable plots were chained together with the lowest scum of female criminals. Men are mixed together in like manner, the murderer and the scholar, the drunken robber, suspected school-teacher, brutish assassins, and young students.

In one of these groups that were passing, I noticed a tall, dejected-looking man, evidently of better grade than his immediate companions, who looked at us with such a gaze of inexpressible sadness that on the impulse of the moment I tossed a piece of silver towards him. As he stooped to pick it up, one of the Cossack guard rushed up, and, giving him a brutal blow, that nearly felled him to the ground, seized the coin, while another rode up to our carriage, which was drawn up at the roadside, and roundly berated the driver.

It must be a terrible region in some portions of Siberia to which these exiles are sent by clemency (?) of the czar. In some parts of the country, notably beyond Tomsk and Ienissa, there are but three months that are not winter, and for three months in the long winter the days are but six hours long, and the labors and terrors of the servitude there, under governors, task-masters, and soldiers (who themselves have been sent there as offenders), although they have from time to time been described, are probably beyond what can be imagined. Once there, it is almost impossible to escape, owing to the long distance to be travelled, as well as the extreme difficulty of procuring proper supplies, passport, or means to preserve life on the journey.

Capital punishment does not prevail in Russia, but it may be considered a worse punishment to be condemned to the slow but sure death in the shaft of quicksilver mines, under the lash of brutal task-masters. Those condemned to these mines are supposed to be of the worst class of convicts, such as thieves and assassins, and their lives rarely last more than ten years, health being exhausted in much less time, as they live, work, and sleep in the mines, and have but two holidays a year, Christmas and Easter.

CHAPTER XIV.

OCCASIONAL stories of the escape of prisoners from Siberia have been told, but I think the most interesting and reliable one of modern date is that written by Mr. William Westall, a year or two ago, in the *Contemporary Review*, of the escape of a political prisoner from Eastern Siberia. Mr. Westall says that, although the difficulty of escape is great from Western Siberia, it is still greater from Eastern, and, although a comparatively easy matter to elude the officers, it is almost impossible to leave the country.

The following is the prisoner's story, in his own words, which Mr. Westall says can be vouched for as being in strict accordance with the truth. All that the writer has done is to omit giving the names of the persons, and to pass over some minor facts which might be of interest to the Russian police. The narrator is a man not more than thirty years old, and of quiet demeanor. To look at him, one would never think that he had passed through such an eventful life.

"I was born at St. Petersburg, and at an early age I entered the Royal Gymnasium of that city, and graduated from that institution at fifteen. I determined to study medicine, and after three years entered the Imperial Pharmacy of St. Catherine in St. Petersburg, and was in the employ of the government. As every one has to serve the government in some way, I determined on this course, as being nearest to my chosen profession. I was assigned to various pharmacies established in Russia by the government, and also served in the medical department attached to the army in the war with the Turcomans. In time I returned to St. Petersburg. I always had a taste for literary pursuits, and contributed some chapters to a book published about five years ago, 'The Four Brothers,' the title of which bore reference to Alexander II. and his three brothers, who led profligate lives, misusing the money wrung from the blood of the people. My article severely censured these princes. These sketches were afterward followed by articles published in 'The Will of the People,' a Nihilistic organ, the numbers of which were issued monthly, and printed in a cellar of St. Petersburg.

"On the 13th of February, 1882, at 2 o'clock in the afternoon, as I was walking home from the Pharmacy St. Catherine, I was accosted by an elderly man, who commanded me to follow him. Thinking he was jesting, I turned to him with some trivial remark, when he told me he was an officer of the secret service, and that I was arrested as a Nihilist; at the same time he showed me his badge. I must have been betrayed by some one, as no one not in sympathy with my Nihilistic ideas knew anything about my actions outside of my position.

"I was taken to the police-station, searched, and all my valuables were confiscated. In less than an hour I was summoned before a court-martial, and sentenced to Siberia, to go with the next body of prisoners. No time was specified as to how long I was to remain in exile. As whatever happens to a Nihilist is at once known by his friends, my father was instantly informed of my arrest. He hurried to the police-station to see me. Of course, my father had much to tell me. We were, however, obliged to carry on our conversation aloud, in Russian. Any secret communication was apparently impossible. My father (God bless him!) overcame this great difficulty. Surrounded as we were by the officers and guard, not a word could be spoken but what they could hear. But he had arranged for this emergency. He had bribed the jailer, for money will do anything in Russia. At a stated signal, the jailer was to come in and attract the attention of the officers. Then my father, in a few words, rapidly spoken, in French, assured me that he had made the fullest arrangements for my escape.

"This interview with my father, which brought some hope to me, only took a few moments. Still, the future was so uncertain, and the chances of escape so difficult, that I quite despaired of ever seeing him again. My father had not the time to give me the full details of the plan, but, still, what he told me I retained in my memory, and recalled on my weary journey afterward even the inflections of his voice.

"My father threw his arms around my neck, whispered a word of consolation in my ears, and we were parted. I was transferred to the city prison, and put in a cell thirty feet under ground. In this horrid dungeon I could not tell night from day. I remember it was cell No. 14 — a celebrated one, as nearly all the political prisoners of the last twenty years have been confined there. I suppose I must have stayed there twenty-four hours, but, as it was pitch-dark, it might have been longer. I was taken from the cell on the 15th of February; my clothes were stripped from my back. Prisoners' clothes, I have every reason to suppose, are stolen by the police, being considered as their perquisites, and sold for their benefit. I was clad in the convict's dress, a long cloak made of the coarsest cloth, resembling a horse-blanket. On my back was painted a yellow diamond, the mark of a political convict. I was ironed hand and foot and placed between two friends of mine, who had been arrested a short time before. In the *étapes* were murderers, thieves, and criminals of every description.

"From St. Petersburg we proceeded by rail to Moscow, thence to Nijni Novgorod, and from there by steamer to Samara. We next took the train to Orenburg, the last town on the Russian frontier. Then we crossed the border into the Kirghiz country. When in Siberia we travelled on foot, though the political prisoners might ride if they wished to. We usually travelled nearly twenty American miles a day. In Siberia our irons were removed; and we were allowed to converse freely among ourselves, a privilege before this denied us. Our guards were generally good-natured, but strict discipline was enforced. All we had to eat was three pounds of Russian black bread a day, made of the coarsest barley. A little salt was given with the bread. Those who had money could purchase brandy or vodki. Our halts on our weary march were made at numerous *kabaks* along the road. A *kabak* is a large barnlike structure, consisting of a bare room with benches around it. In entering one of these places there is a general rush for the benches. Those who are weak and ill, or are not lucky enough to get a bench, pass the night in the middle of the floor.

"The first important town we reached in Siberia was Tobolsk, and from there we pushed on to Tomsk, which was to have been our last station. The time occupied in going so far had been fully two months, and on our weary journey we had tramped nearly two thousand miles. During all this time, you can well imagine, I sometimes lost courage and despaired of ever being rescued.

"Now comes the most interesting part of my story. We did not go into the town of Tomsk, but stopped at a *kabak* about twenty miles outside of the place. While in the *kabak* I noticed a man who acted as if he were drunk. This person asked us who was going to treat. We told him we had no money. 'Well,' said he, 'I'll treat you.' While we were drinking some vodki, the man managed to tell us who he was, for he was so disguised that it was impossible for us to recognize him. It was a friend, an engineer, the man my father had employed to save me. He had been in Tomsk, so he told us, some time, and had enlisted as a blacksmith. A portion of his duty was to shackle and unshackle the prisoners. He told us we must ask permission of the guards to take a bath.

"Baths in Russia and Siberia are far different from those in America. Nearly every peasant's house has its bath. This consists of a small out-house in which stones are heated red-hot and water thrown over them. The bather stands in the vapor. Consent to bathe was granted us. After we had finished our bath, my friend replaced our irons, but failed to lock them. While we were in the bath, the blacksmith had plied the officers and guards with so much vodki that they all were in a kind of half-drunken stupor. The man who examined our irons was too much fuddled to notice that they were not locked.

"We lay down and kept perfectly still till midnight. Then, quietly slipping our irons, we stole softly out of the *kabak*, running as hard as we could until we were out of sight of the house. We made for a small ravine near the *kabak*. Here my rescuer was waiting for us. He had secured a horse and wagon. We scrambled into the wagon, and, lashing the horse, madly plunged into the densest part of the forest. After going along at a breakneck speed for about ten miles, we stopped the horse and stayed in the forest till morning.

"There was a change of clothes in the wagon, and we threw aside our convict garb and assumed the uniform of Russian officers. While on our way to Tomsk we heard a terrific sound of trampling hoofs, and were in momentary fear of being overtaken. We thought it might be a troop of Cossacks. Unfortunately for us, the animal which pulled our wagon was a mare, and a herd of wild horses had scented her. We turned the animal loose, when, rejoicing at her freedom, she ran away with the rest of her newly found friends. We burned our wagon and proceeded on our way to Tomsk on foot. Here we remained only long enough to hurry off in the next post to Yeniseisk. Up the Yenisei River we took a canal-boat to Techoul-Kora.

"I forgot to state that all prisoners in Russia have one-half their heads shaved. So, while hiding in the forest around Tomsk, we took turns in cutting one another's hair. How different was our journey homeward! With plenty of money, given us by our rescuer, we took the fastest boats and had the speediest horses. If we happened to pass a fortress or band of prisoners, the officers saluted us, and the peasants treated us as if we were the truest friends the czar ever had. From Techoul-Kora we made our way back to Russia. As soon as we crossed the border, we changed our dress to that of civilians. I was disguised as a coachman. In Russia great care had to be taken. We travelled only on the most unfrequented roads, and associated with no one whom we did not know to be friendly to our cause. After reaching Ekaterinburg we crossed the Ural Mountains to Kazan, where I parted from my friends and the engineer. Picture to yourself the sorrow of leaving the man who had risked his life to save ours. It was easy enough to travel in Russia; any one can do that, providing he has plenty of money.

"From Nijni Novgorod I went to Vilna, a small town in Poland, where, to my intense delight, I met my father. He told me that all his fortune had been confiscated by the government, and that I must leave the country at once. Giving me a small sum of money, my gold watch and chain, he bade me good-bye. From Vilna I went to Koons, where I took a steamer on the Niemen River to Judgeborg, a small town in Poland, only twenty miles from Germany. Now the question was, how was I to get out of Russia without a passport? That difficulty was easily overcome. There are any number of people who, for the sum of from three to five roubles, will smuggle you across, though you stand in constant danger of being captured by a kind of mounted police, whose duty it is to guard the boundary line.

"After running some great risks in Judgeborg, I finally came across one of these people whom I thought could aid me in getting out of the blackest country on the face of the earth. The man was to meet me at 12 o'clock at night. I went to bed and stayed there till nearly the appointed hour. Then rising and dressing myself, I left the house. I found my wagoner waiting for me. These men secure fourteen days' passes from the government, which allows them to take travellers and baggage into Germany. During my drive all my former adventures, even to the simplest incidents of my childhood, were vividly recalled to my mind. I rejoiced at leaving Russia, but thought of my father, mother, sisters, brothers, and friends, whom I might never see again.

"The Russian border is separated from Germany by a narrow creek, not wider than an ordinary room. My preozschick ordered me to get out of the wagon. He alighted first, taking the precaution of lying flat on the road. He placed his ear to the ground so as to listen if there was not an obejschick in the neighborhood. Not hearing any sound, he told me to push on. Leaping across the creek, I was for the first time a free man, though not yet entirely out of the clutches of the Russian government. I ran as fast as my legs would carry me, when suddenly I stopped. Directly in front of me I saw a man. He was lying flat on his back. Good God! He was a police guard. There he lay, sleeping soundly, holding his horse's bridle, the horse quietly cropping the grass. The animal had his head turned away from me. The man must have been drunk. Drawing my knife, the only weapon I had, I made up my mind that it was a question of life or death. I jumped over the body of the prostrate man. Had he risen from his sleep or made a motion to stop me, I should have tried to have given him a death-thrust with my knife.

"How far I ran I don't know, but in my confusion I took the wrong road and ran in a circle almost to the Russian border. I was about to enter the guard-house, a large white building, which bore some resemblance to a hotel my wagoner had directed me to. I had nearly reached the building when, on the entrance, I espied, above the door, the Russian arms. Fortunately, it was early in the morning, and no one was awake. I can assure you I lost no time in regaining the road. After a while I reached the hotel I was seeking. I had barely strength enough to knock at the door, and when I got inside I had to be assisted to my room. I travelled through various small towns in Germany until I reached Berlin. I intended staying in Germany, but, as I could get no work in my profession, I went to Havre. Here my means were exhausted. I pawned my watch, and, hearing that there would be a steamer for New York, I made up my mind to try my fortune in America, bought a steerage ticket, and landed in New York City in April, 1883, with seventeen dollars in my pocket."

It is generally understood that many of the political arrests in Russia and banishments to Siberia have been quietly and secretly done by the government, in some cases, as asserted, the victims disappearing so suddenly as to leave no clew, even to friends and relatives, of their whereabouts.

The worst feature of some of these political arrests is that many who are but suspected of conspiracy against the government are subjected to imprisonment and often have the greatest difficulty in communicating with their friends, while others who have innocently transacted business with Nihilists or conspirators, not knowing them as such, are torn from home and friends, and, if we can believe English accounts, given no opportunity to know what charges are made against them or opportunity to disprove them.

A recent case was recorded by a correspondent of the *Levant Herald* of the strange meeting of a learned professor in the wilds of Siberia by one of his former students, who, as a civil engineer, was in Central Asia for some time.

The monotony of his residence in those remote provinces was broken by an occasional hunting expedition into Siberia. On one of these trapping expeditions, which included a younger member of one of the grand-ducal families, the party was one evening belated in a pine-forest and at some distance from the day's bivouac. They were utterly astray. A stentorian view-halloo, reverberating through the silent recesses of the forest-depths, brought to the assistance and guidance of the party a wood-cutter — an old man, of some threescore years, with tangled locks, coarse caftan, and bark-swathed feet. Under the old man's guidance, the party found a rude hut, a charcoal fire, and some simple cooking-utensils.

The engineer noticed that the old wood-cutter, when unobserved, scanned his face rather attentively. He took a quiet opportunity of asking the old man if he observed in him any resemblance to some one he had previously known.

"A very strong resemblance," was the reply. "Were you not some fifteen years ago a student of the Richelevski Gymnase in Odessa?"

The engineer answered affirmatively.

"And do you remember Professor ——?"

"Certainly; he was a man beloved by every student in his class. I shall always remember kindly the amiable and learned professor who disappeared so suddenly and mysteriously from Odessa. But what do you know of him?"

The old wood-cutter for the first time smiled. The heavy moustache and beard had hidden the lines of the mouth in repose. The young engineer had not forgotten the peculiarly sad sweetness of his old professor's smile. The ragged and picturesque wood-cutter and the former learned professor of Sanscrit and comparative philology were the same.

"The rencontre," continues the correspondent, "was, under the circumstances, naturally at once both pleasing and painful to my friend, to whose immediate and anxious inquiries the old man replied sadly: —

"'All God's will, my boy. As to the suddenness and mystery of my disappearance from Odessa, the secret police might have explained. Nothing beyond an unfounded suspicion of disaffection to our Little Father and a preposterous charge of disseminating a revolutionary doctrine have sent me to this life-long banishment. But I do not repine. I have sufficient philosophy left to apply myself to the felling of pine-trees with the same zest as that with which I formerly delighted to pursue a knotty philological problem.

"'Am I not wise in my generation and old age? I am deprived of the sight and companionship of old friends, but God gives me health and a portion of contentment. My masters pay me with but few unkind words and two roubles a week. My old Odessa pupils paid me six roubles an hour. But what of that? I have sufficient. Sometimes old memories draw tightly round the heart and give me infinite pain. Then I swing my heavy adze with greater force, and endeavor to forget. It is to me a joy to look upon the still youthful face of my old pupil, but do not probe my heart, child. I ask you not to speak to me at parting. You were always obedient, and you hear me. God keep you! Good-bye!'"

The old man would not allow the friend to convey

any messages to relatives or acquaintances, who, he said, had probably long since forgotten his existence, and he would not disturb dead memories, so that nothing could be done beyond an affectionate pressure of the hand, without a word, at leave-taking.

How many others are there like the old professor, men also of birth, breeding, and brilliant intellectual parts, languishing out their lives in the dreary wilds of Siberia for a baseless suspicion? The reflection is saddening, and it also comes home to us after inspecting the laboriously cut and elegantly carved pillars of churches, from stone of almost adamantine hardness, pedestals, stone steps, pediments, columns, and other work from Siberian quarries.

For one thinks that this beautiful work, that represents years of painful and careful application, may have been wrought with aching hearts and washed by the hopeless tears of those longing for the sight of loved ones and far distant home.

On the other hand, portions of Siberia are represented as flourishing and even pleasant places for the average Russian to live in, and with better opportunities than are afforded in the generality of Russian villages. But while not much can be said in praise of the villages of Russian peasants, it is a fact among all peoples that it is rare that any compensation can be found for the deprivation of one's liberty.

CHAPTER XV.

HAVING occasion to make a remittance to a friend in Germany while I was in Moscow, I was about to enclose a ten-pound note in my letter, when I was cautioned not to do so, as there is a law forbidding the transportation of any money into or out of the kingdom through the mails, and post-office officials have authority to open letters which they suspect and seize any money they may find therein, one-third going to the government and two-thirds to the official. All remittances, therefore, to ensure safety, must be made by means of bankers' drafts. I presume this is to enable the government to keep track of funds received or expended for plots or conspiracies, but that such regulation exists it is fortunate for the tourist to know, lest he unwittingly contribute to the funds of some government official in the post-office department. The only way to get foreign newspapers in Russia is to have them mailed to your consul or minister; at the Russian post-offices they will be examined on arrival, and all objectionable passages blacked out of them as before described.

It is a ride of about five miles out to the Simonof Monastery, one of the richest and most important monastic institutions in the empire, and founded here about the year 1390. It is a large and beautiful extent of ground, enclosing dormitories, chapels, little houses with gay gardens, and other buildings, including no less than six churches within its walls. The central church, surmounted by five great cupolas, has a sort of semi-Chinese or Saracenic aspect, and the old red walls, the huge monastic gate, and the beautiful avenue of trees gave a very picturesque aspect to the scene.

This monastery, in olden times, was a regular feudal institution, owning numerous villages and enabled to call into the field a regular army of its own of over twelve thousand serfs about the year 1764. It has had a notable history, having been conquered and sacked by invading Lithuanians and Poles in 1612, made a plague hospital in 1771, suppressed in 1778, and restored in 1795, to be again partially destroyed in 1812.

We drove into the enclosure, and, after some difficulty, our guide found a man in charge, but, it being just 12 o'clock, priests, monks, and all were asleep, and, like the Spaniards and Italians, had all retired for noon siesta and would not be awake and about for two or three hours. The ever and all-powerful roubles, however, brought out a long-robed and bearded official from his slumbers, who showed us about the Church of the Assumption, and sleepily descanted upon the altar-screen, the great gilt cupola, and the two towers, one 85 and the other 125 feet high. In the sacristy were the rich robes, heavy with gold embroidery — so heavy, indeed, that it would seem like doing penance to wear them any length of time.

Here also were rich cups, huge gold tureens or vessels, and other ecclesiastical treasures, including the gospels bound in gold and ornamented with precious stones — which seems to have been a favorite present of monarchs to monasteries. This one was given by Mary, the daughter of Alexis.

The chief object for which the monastery is visited,

however, is to ascend the bell-tower, three hundred and thirty feet high, where, looking out through a trap-door in the very top of the cupola, you have a magnificent panoramic view of Moscow and the surrounding country, and again realize what an important part the walled-in Kremlin, beautiful monastery grounds, the numerous parti-colored roofs and spires, gilded domes and glittering steeples, play in presenting a novel and thoroughly foreign, as well as picturesque, view to the eye of the American tourist.

This monastery is on the edge of a steep rise of ground, and in quite an advantageous and commanding position, and is approached by a narrow road between its walls and the cliff-side; its central gate, under the great bell-tower, is kept closed, and the circle of towers on the walls were of service in resisting some severe sieges years ago.

On our way back we pass another great monastery, that of the New Redeemer, surrounded by high walls which enclose several churches within their limits. The monastery was plundered by Napoleon's soldiers, and its antique stone walls date back to 1642. The belfry, like that of the Simonof, is a striking object and rises to the height of 235 feet. Near here are the ruins of a beautiful arch or gate, said to be the entrance to a former archiepiscopal palace.

But we soon leave the country behind, and, nearing the city, we ride along beside the river and in sight of a beautiful view of the Kremlin from that side, showing the battlemented walls, huge buildings, turreted towers, and glittering spires, all grouped above us in the sunlight, strikingly reminding one of Martin's picture of tier above tier of palaces that surrounded Satan as: —

> "High on a throne of royal state, which far
> Outshone the wealth of Ormus or of Ind,
> Or where the gorgeous East with richest hand
> Showers on her kings barbaric pearls and gold,
> Satan exalted sat."

The Romanoff House, which all tourists are expected to visit as the former residence of the Romanoffs, the present royal family of Russia, is simply a restoration of the ancient building of 1613, in which the first Romanoff czar was born. The exterior walls are said to be the same, but the interior was restored and fitted up in 1858, in the style of a Russian gentleman's house of the sixteenth and seventeenth centuries, and as such the interior, with its massive and cumbersome fittings and appliances, is a curiosity and sort of ancient art-museum.

The building is four stories in height, and the different rooms, reached by narrow stairways, are furnished in the antique Russian style. The great chamber has a sort of Gothic roof, richly decorated, and in this room were kept many curious and massive pieces of ancient furniture and plate; some of the latter formerly belonging to the family is of massive silver richly wrought. A great German stove, with its colored tiles, was the heating apparatus of the apartment. Then there was the nursery, with its clumsy, great, heavy cradles and rude chairs for children of the period, their wooden dolls and primers, and in the bedchamber the ceiling and walls were all beautifully carved in wood, in various designs, and the old, heavy four-post bedstead and huge chairs, I presume, were Russian antique furniture, and in a glass case was a long robe and a pair of slippers, said to be those of the first czar and czarina of the Romanoffs. The whole is a collection of ancient domestic art, illustrative of the manner and customs of domestic life when the Romanoffs first came into power.

The numerous curious relics that are presented relating to the former sovereigns of Russia — in fact, the many interesting objects connected with the past history of the empire, of which the average American has so superficial a knowledge — cause him to realize his ignorance in that respect, and create a desire, as in my case, to go home and more thoroughly read up the history of Russia and its people.

More than once did I meet tourists who, like myself, were making but a brief visit to the country, who expressed their wonder and surprise at what (as an American of considerable experience as a tourist expressed it) " a tremendous amount to see there was in St. Petersburg and Moscow."

That there is much to interest the intelligent traveller may be gathered from these very sketchy descriptions of only the leading sights seen, and jotted down after a long day's work visiting them, and the traveller visiting St. Petersburg and Moscow for the first time will find that there is far more to see and more time required to do it than he imagined at the outset.

Were it not for diary and note-book, how palaces, churches, and monasteries would become mixed up in one's memory, and, after having visited two or three churches, a certain general similarity seems to strike one, and, in the endeavor to give a pen-picture of one after another of these grand temples to the Most High in this distant land, the impression naturally forces itself into my mind that such description in Russia can in no degree be so interesting as that of an old English abbey, for instance, that has figured in history, romance, and story, till generation after generation had heard, dreamed, and imagined of it, and longed to look upon the crumbling walls or stand upon the ground where have been enacted the scenes sung of by poets, illustrated by painters, or represented upon the stage.

But rarely visited as Russia is by the rush of pleasure-seekers abroad, I have wondered that such as do go and who write about it do not give us a little more of the actual detail of description, which is of so much service to those who come after. This I have endeavored to do, at the risk of being tedious, although mention of the contents of church after church and palace after palace becomes something like an inventory of possessions.

The Royal Palace at Moscow is really quite a modern affair, being finished about thirty-five years ago. The interior is magnificent, the apartments being distinguished for their beauty and grandeur. You first pass through a grand entrance and vestibule supported by a series of beautiful monoliths of gray marble, and on through beautifully decorated corridors to what are known as the royal apartments, which are a series of elegant and richly furnished rooms decorated with different-colored silk hangings. The empress' drawing-room is furnished in beautiful white silk and gold, her cabinet in a dark ruby-colored silk, and her bathroom is rich in elegant marble, with a superb malachite mantel-piece.

Then there are the halls and antechambers, as usual in palaces, richly gilded and frescoed, but containing nothing of note till we entered one known as the Emperor's Cabinet, in which were paintings of the entrance of the French into Moscow, and their retreat, also views of the battles of Borodino and Smolensk. The Russians like to keep prominently in mind the defeat of the hitherto invincible chieftain who dared to invade their territory and despoil their holy city. A statuette in bronze of Napoleon stands in the middle of the room, as if to say, This is the man whose invading battalions were hurled back, beaten, and destroyed by Russian valor (and Russia's winter).

A glance at a room of regimental standards which belong to the different regiments of the Russian army, and we step out to the grand granite staircase that leads to the state apartments. Here, on the great circular landing round the gallery at the head of the staircase, is a fine and spirited battle-piece, representing a victory of the Russians over the Tartars.

We passed from here into a splendid apartment, 200 feet long, 68 wide, and about sixty feet in height, elegantly decorated. The military order of St. George was founded by Catherine II., in 1769, and the names of all the individuals and regiments that have ever been decorated with the order are inscribed upon the marble walls of this apartment, in golden letters, and number thousands.

The grand columns of this hall are a delusion, being formed of zinc, but have a fine and imposing appearance. They are surmounted by figures bearing shields, upon which are inscriptions of Russian victories. The superb vases and candelabra are notable features of this room. The candelabra sustain about three thousand five hundred lights. The furniture and fittings of this grand hall are of the colors of the order of St. George, black and orange.

Another magnificent hall in the palace is that known as the hall of St. Andrew, an order of knighthood that was founded by Peter I., in 1698.

In this hall, which is 160 feet long by 68 wide, is a magnificent royal throne, and the whole is furnished and hung with blue silk, the color of this order of knighthood; it is also decorated with numerous coats-of-arms and knightly devices, which I supposed to be those of distinguished knights, but which turned out, on inquiry, to be the arms of different provinces of the empire.

Still another grand hall, dedicated to another order of knighthood, is that of St. Alexander Nevsky, a hall 150 feet long and about seventy wide, lighted by four thousand five hundred candles. This order of knighthood was founded by that industrious sovereign, Catherine II., in 1725, and, its colors being pink, the room is gorgeous in pink and gold decorations.

There are six great pictures here representing scenes in the life of the saint of the order. One is a spirited representation of a battle on the ice, another a marriage-scene, and a third a triumphal entry into some city; these are the most remarkable.

After these grand apartments, that of St. Catherine, 68 feet by 45, looks small, and, sated with sight-seeing of this description, you pass through the great state drawing-room with its rich furniture, the state bed-room, gorgeous with mosaic work and jasper mantel-piece, and then out through a pretty garden to other apartments, only one of which we looked into, a dining-room hung with tapestry representing scenes in the life of Don Quixote.

There were other halls, of no special note, but we now entered an older part of the structure, known as the Granite Palace; we were shown the celebrated "Red Staircase," a structure famous as being the scene of many noted events in Russian history.

From the top of this staircase the czars were wont to show themselves to the people, and here is the scene of one of the acts of that cruel tyrant, John the Terrible, who struck his sharp, iron-pointed staff into the foot of a messenger bringing him unfavorable news, and held him thus pinned to the floor while he read the despatches. From these steps rebels, pretenders to the crown, unpopular rulers, and others have been hurled upon the pikes of the soldiery below, or seized, dragged down, and cut to pieces, and up these steps the victorious Napoleon and his marshals mounted to take possession of the Kremlin.

Next came the room where coronation banquets are served — an apartment with a huge column in the centre, from which spring vaulted arches.

Here the emperor dines, with his nobles, after the ceremony of coronation. The great theatrical-looking chairs upon a dais at one end of the apartment mark the position of the emperor, who appears here in his royal robes, and none but crowned heads are allowed at his table, and no women admitted to the hall. A window opposite the throne, high up in the wall, marks the spot where a few ladies of high rank may have an opportunity of looking in upon the royal banquet. The imperial plate used at these banquets is preserved here in glass cases, and forms a perfect museum of elegant design and workmanship, ancient and modern, of the silver-smith's art.

It seems here in Moscow that they have something everywhere to show you to recall the name of Napoleon and his invasion. Here is pointed out the point of his entrance into the city; there the point of departure; here are his camp-bedsteads, and there the church which he plundered and stabled horses in; here are shown captured standards, the celebrated French eagles, and there is evident pride in the disaster to the invading force, which is ascribed to the invincible character of the Russian soldiers, and little or no credit is given to the Russian winter, which had so much to do with the annihilation of the retreating host that went down by thousands before the whirling snow-wreaths.

The cannon that were taken from the retiring enemy are pointed to proudly as trophies, many of which were doubtless captured in the fierce charges of the Cossacks upon the thinned and exhausted rear-guard as they painfully urged their way back over barren wastes, chilled and exhausted with the fierce blasts of winter that had overtaken them, and others by scores were, as we know, abandoned for lack of horses to drag or men to man them.

The tactics of the Russian generals, after the battle of Borodino and subsequent advance of Napoleon, proved most successful, and, instead of entering a populated city and dictating terms to the Russian people, who should humbly come to him suing for peace, and proffering an indemnity, the invader found, to his mortification, that the population had fled. None remained save convicts, whom the Russians had liberated from the prisons, and some of the most miserable of the lowest class, who were unable to leave.

The holy city was given up to be sacrificed for the benefit of the empire. Negotiations were refused, propositions for treaty and armistice disregarded by the Russian generals, and, after a month's stay, the invading army — 150,000 men, 50,000 horses, and 500 pieces of cannon — started on its return, stretching away from burning Moscow in three great columns over the open country, followed by forty thousand stragglers and a huge train of wagons bearing captured booty. When this mighty host started, then the Muscovite commanders grimly announced that their campaign had just begun. How disastrous it was to the French emperor, the history of the retreat from Moscow attests.

The travellers' stories about the fair of Nijni Novgorod, until quite recently, have given one to understand that the place during the fair was a regular congress of nations. Imagination revelled from these descriptions, picturing trains of camels bearing their spicy loads from the East; turbaned Turks seated upon rich carpets, puffing chibouks or the fragrant hubble-bubble, with embroidered slippers and rich stuffs for sale; Arabs of the desert; crowds of pig-tailed Chinese, with their tea-chests; tall, sedate Persians, or curious Kalmucks, Copts, Tartars, and Greeks mixed all together in a kaleidoscopic and picturesque confusion, engaged in bartering the richest products of their respective countries.

Perhaps in the old times of the fair, when men brought their merchandise on camels and by caravan trains (for it dates back to 1366), this may have been to a certain degree correct; but modern improvements and the railroad line to Moscow, which puts the fair in direct communication with the other lines of railway and with all parts of Europe, have wrought a vast change.

The distance from Moscow to Nijni, which is said to be the centre of European Russia, is 273 miles, and the price in a first-class railway carriage is fifteen roubles, and we were told that the journey would be accomplished in thirteen hours, but we were really fourteen hours and a half accomplishing it. The train left at 8 at night and we arrived at 10:30 next morning.

The sleeping-cars on this route are not so comfortable as those between St. Petersburg and Moscow. The contrivance for sleeping consists in the pulling-out of a slide from beneath the seat to meet one from the opposite seat. Then, with the cushions for a couch, and your wraps, you make yourself tolerably comfortable for the night.

As we found that the car-compartments held five, and there being but three in our party, we found it contributed to our comfort to have the conductor or guard interviewed previous to starting from Moscow, which insured us the compartment exclusively for our own use and free from any intrusion during the journey. A very good breakfast of chops, eggs, coffee, and excellent French rolls was had at the Nijni station, costing about a rouble and a half (seventy-five cents) each, and we were ready for the drosky, with its impatient steeds and long-robed driver, that was awaiting us.

The best way to proceed in sight-seeing at Nijni is to breakfast, as we did, at the railway station immediately on arrival, after which to engage a good two-horse carriage and driver for the day, and proceed at once with your guide to the fair-grounds and points of interest.

CHAPTER XVI.

NIJNI NOVGOROD (Lower Novgorod) is so called to distinguish it from Novgorod the Great, an old and celebrated city in Russia, said to be the cradle of the Russian empire, and which once covered an area of forty miles, and was a place of immense wealth. But it is Nijni Novgorod that the traveller has heard most of and desires to see.

Nijni is an older town than Moscow, and from its peculiar position admirably adapted for a distributing-point or sort of grand depot for the merchandise of Central Asia, the East, and the vast region of Siberia, which is to be sent from here to the West, and *vice versa*. It is, in fact, a sort of connecting commercial link between the continents of Europe and Asia, a rendezvous of the merchants of both continents. The town is spread over a large amount of territory, but has, I am told, but fifty thousand inhabitants. It is situated at the junction of the Volga and Oka rivers, and the fair is held upon a great tract of land immediately between these two streams.

These two rivers are among the largest in Russia, the Volga having a course of over twenty-three hundred miles. The Oka is a tributary of eight hundred and fifty miles, and flows into the Volga. Nijni occupies a geographical point peculiarly favorable for a commercial port, being at the centre of the water-communication that joins the Black and Caspian seas with the White and Baltic seas, a grand water-highway during the summer season.

The pavements in Nijni are as abominable as they well can be, and our ride through the town, on our way to the fair, gave us a view of quite a miscellaneous character. We passed all manner of cheap shops and bazaars, strings of wretchedly made wagons loaded with all kinds of merchandise, swarms of filthy, ragged laborers, mostly Tartars, besides filthy, sheepskin-clad Russians, great warehouses, cheap restaurants, and swarms of droskies. No well dressed people were seen in the streets, and rarely any women except Tartars, whom you detect by their features or their long yellow boots as they raise their dresses to cross the dusty or muddy streets, blind beggars, and others that are not blind.

A Russian beggar, by the bye, is a most repulsive object, clad in a perfect mass of rags or sheepskins, that cause you to wonder how they hold together, his legs and feet bound with rags and straw covering, his repulsive, corrugated, unwashed face almost hidden in a mass of matted, unkempt hair of head and beard; he holds out a hand crusted with the dirt of years, and begs a trifle in the name of the saints. But he is an object in every way so repugnant that he generally gets a wide berth from European or American visitors.

The Russian religious pilgrim is another disgusting object. Clad in sheepskins and rags, that are dust-covered and filthy from his long journey from the interior, on his way to some noted shrine or church, to fulfil some vow made to saints or to perform some penance, he trudges on with his feet protected by swathing of soft bark and rags, and a wallet hanging about his neck containing scraps of food that he has begged. He exudes an odor of sanctity that could well be dispensed with. When he elbows his way into the crowded cathedral to perform his devotions, other worshippers give way to him with promptitude.

Our drive carried us along the river-bank for some little distance, when we descended, crossed a bridge, and were at once in the limits of the fair. That portion to which you are first taken gives you the impression of anything but the popular idea of a fair. It appears like a collection of vast quantities of merchandise in bulk, so vast that you wonder how it ever could have got there, and how it ever will be taken away. But go up, as you will, on the high land or terrace above, and look down upon the River Volga, stretching away in the distance till it becomes a mere steel-like ribbon in the sunlight, and the Oka on the other side, and you will get some idea of the enormous commerce of the empire.

More than a hundred and fifty great freight-steamers were moored at the banks or gliding to and fro; huge bateaux, piled with bales, casks, boxes, and hogsheads of merchandise, were being propelled by steam-tugs from point to point; the rivers were black with heavily laden craft, of every description, as far as the eye could reach. There were ten miles of wharf on the two rivers, and they and the great plain occupied by the fair were piled with every kind of merchandise.

The iron-market was the first portion of the fair we drove through — a space of flat, dusty plain, with the heavy merchandise displayed on either side of the road that ran through it. There were great heaps of Russian sheet-iron, and Tartar laborers loading it upon teams, the perspiration running in streams down their faces and half-naked bodies; then huge heaps of bar-iron, of every kind I had ever seen, and much that I had never seen; pig-iron, iron in bundles, iron in ingots, a great lot of every kind of iron anchors.

It was iron on every side of us — the ringing of bars as they were loaded into the vehicles, the crash of sheet-iron piled in great heaps, like huge lots of iron manuscripts, and the thud of the pig-iron being tossed into clumsy carts, were the features of this place. We saw heaps of the celebrated Russian iron, the secret of the manufacture of which has long been confined to Russia.

This secret, however, has been recently discovered, and by an American, who obtained it, of course, surreptitiously, and at great personal risk. The name of the adventurous individual is Mr. William Rogers, of Pennsylvania, who, about eighteen years ago, was sent out, as state geologist, to Russia, and bearing credentials to the minister at St. Petersburg.

As long as he confined his explorations to the mines, he attracted little or no suspicion; but as soon as he set his foot inside the iron-mills of Princess Demidoff, he was subjected to the most vigilant espionage. It must be remembered that the men in the mills who know the secret of making Russian iron are never allowed to quit the mills. With the special study he had made of iron-making before going to Russia, he was not long in discovering the much-coveted secret, though he had much trouble to evade suspicion. Had he been detected, he might have been forced to remain in Siberia the rest of his life; but he was not.

And now a mill is in process of construction at Freeport, a little town about thirty miles north of Pittsburg, Pa., for the manufacture of this iron; and it will be the first Russian-iron mill built outside of Siberia. An imitation of Russian iron has been made in this country for some time, but it is not proof against rust. Imperviousness to rust is the test of genuine Russian iron.

Leaving the iron quarter and its throngs of perspiring laborers, we drove into another division of the plain. Here the scene changed, and we were in the midst of bells of every description, from the small one that would have sounded musical in a school-house belfry, to the huge, deep-toned giant that would have fitted the tower of St. Isaac's or St. Peter's.

Next we were whirled into a space where were mountains of bales of wool and cotton, on either side. Here and there were rude shanties, bearing signs that told they were the counting-houses or headquarters of merchants of St. Petersburg, Moscow, Odessa, or other Russian cities, and in which, during the day, were to be found their representatives, who remain here during the fair to look after their interests. Then from a broad, plain-like space of ground, as we approached it, came that fragrant perfume that told of the great tea-quarter of the fair, and we rode through vast squares, formed of thousands and thousands of tea-chests. Did we see Chinamen here? Not one.

In this quarter different cargoes, or, maybe, different varieties, of tea are piled, forming great hollow squares, with one side open towards the roadway. Within, seated upon a rude bench, with a great wooden tub before them, were two men, dressed in the Russian merchant-costumes. One held a large book, in which entries were made of the result of the inspection of the other of the tea which passed before them.

This was done something in this fashion. Two laborers brought the chest to a broad piece of cloth, that was spread before the inspectors, and set it down;

another pierced the chest with a single blow of his long, sharp tea-sampler or trier, drawing it forth filled with the fragrant herb, and presented it to one of the inspectors, who passed it rapidly beneath his nostrils, and, with a deep inhalation, gave it a critical glance. Then he spoke a word to the man with the book, who checked it off, and indicated to two other laborers to pile it right, left, or centre, where that of its quality was deposited. A man with a cork or bung immediately stopped the sample-hole, and the chest was seized and carried to its proper position. The samples drawn were thrown into the receptacle in front of the inspectors.

In another square were men sampling and evidently bargaining for purchases; in a third, load after load was being carried away. The whole atmosphere was redolent of tea and that peculiar sort of indescribable sandal-wood scent that one notices on entering a Chinese tea and curiosity shop.

All the chests have either coverings of matting or hides to protect them. The laborers here are principally Tartars. They live any way, camp out during the season in the rudest of huts made of a few boards and old tea-mattings; curl themselves up at night on a few old tea-mattings and a heap of dried grass and sleep on the ground. The town, where cheap tea, vodki, and beer can be had, is but a short distance from the place, and they frequent it at night or when not at work, and lead a sort of Bohemian life during the season. The agents of the tea-merchants also live in this quarter. They have little cabins, about twenty feet square, built of boards, covered with tea-matting; inside, the floor is covered with the same matting, and at the side were two bunks for the sleepers. A rude table, a couple of chairs, and other articles such as we are accustomed to see in a hunter's camp, completed the outfit.

Tea appears to be one of the most important articles of merchandise at Nijni, and of the finer qualities about sixteen millions of pounds are brought to Russia annually. Throughout Russia and Central Asia, tea seems to be as a beverage to the natives what beer is to the Germans.

It is drunk at the fair by all nationalities, even the Moslems; the poorer classes of Tartars and laborers contenting themselves with the cheap brick-tea, so called from its being moistened and pressed into that form for convenience of transportation. The Russians say the English do not drink the best tea, because they will not pay for the best grades.

Bokhara sends merchandise by camel-train, as of old, to this fair; some of the trains coming a thousand miles, and starting in the spring on a six-weeks journey to reach it. These caravans bring cotton, silk, and that black, curly, and glossy fur, real black astrakhan, the skin of a jet-black curly lamb; also rice, wheat, and barley, woven fabrics, and dried fruits.

Merchandise of a very different character was that in the horse department, where were draught and other horses, chiefly for laboring purposes, but in great variety, in their different sheds, or being run up and down before them in view of probable purchasers. Here there were clouds of dust, a clatter of hoofs, a shouting of grooms, and a neighing of steeds. Count Orloff, who presented the famous diamond, the largest in Europe, to the Empress Catherine II., was much interested and did much towards improving the breed of Russian horses; hence, most horses of good blood in Russia are styled Orloff horses. The type of horse most frequently seen in St. Petersburg and Moscow is solidly built, has a large head and neck, large legs, and is far less graceful in action than the steeds one sees in England and America. The prevailing color is black. The best carriage-horses seemed to be stallions; they look stylish, trot fast, and appear to be quiet and docile. They certainly are splendid animals for use in sight-seeing about St. Petersburg, Moscow, and the suburbs, for they keep going from morning till night upon a fast trot, from point to point, and will conclude, as in our experience, with a journey out seven miles from the city and return without a symptom of fatigue or exertion.

In Russia, as in America, much more interest is taken in trotting than in running races. I am unable to say how the speed of Russian trotters compares with American fast horses, but the Russian racer looks too heavy in build to accomplish a mile in the time that it has been done by our clean-limbed coursers. The carriage used in trotting races in Russia is a singular-looking affair. It consists of four wheels of about the size of those of an American buggy, and from one axle to the other is a board, thickly padded and covered with leather; this board forms the seat for the driver, and, as his feet swing without support, the sensation must be similar to that experienced in riding upon a rail. Russian horses have frequently been taken to Paris to compete with trotting horses from Normandy on the race-track laid out in the Bois de Boulogne just outside of the running race-track, but the trial has ended in the triumph of the Normans over their Russian competitors. It is a curious fact that Russians, notorious for fast driving, have no bells on their horses in winter. Accidents frequently occur from this cause.

From the horse-marts we passed on again and found ourselves in a section more like a regular fair. It was a collection of nuts, dates, dried fruits, and everything of that sort, in huge heaps, with broad display of samples, that might be purchased at retail of tall semi-Turkish-costumed individuals.

There were almonds, dates, figs, Rahat Lakoum (fig-paste), Turkish sweetmeats, etc., nor were these all eastern goods, for there were bags of Castanea nuts, heaps of "English walnuts," pecan-nuts, raisins and other dried fruits. From here stretched out a long string of shops, a sort of cheap bazaar, where were various silks, dry-goods, etc., but such as were no novelty, and could be seen in greater variety and to greater advantage in London and Paris, and some of the Eastern fabrics, as well as the furs in the furrier section, could be bought cheaper, and with a greater certainty of one's not being cheated, in London than here.

In the section devoted to Persian goods were magnificent rugs and carpets, which two obliging dark-skinned attendants brought forth and spread upon a plot of hardened earth in front of their booths, in which were heaped huge piles of goods of gorgeous dyes. I coveted one, rich, antique, soft as dressed chamois-skin, with the hues blending as beautifully as the tints of an oil-painting, which the Persian, Armenian, or Greek — I thought him the latter, from his fez, baggy trousers, and red slippers — assured me in French was "bon marché véritable," direct from a Turkish person of distinction, etc.

The problem of getting the article through various custom-houses to the United States, and the difficulty of knowing whether you are being cheated or not, stands in the way of European and American tourists here.

Our guide informed us that Turkish rugs for this fair were manufactured in France, as well as Turkish pipes, dress-stuffs, and even Circassian chain-armor, helmets, and shields; besides, Persian articles that have never seen that country, made in France and Belgium, are sold here every year, and one must have his wits about him in making purchases, both as to price and genuineness of the articles offered.

It would be too tiresome and prosy to the reader to describe great collections of grindstones from the Ural Mountains, huge casks of fish and barrels of herring from Astrakhan, enormous quantities of petroleum, piles of hides, huge heaps of cotton from Bokhara, and one section that glittered with all kinds of copper vessels, including a large collection of the celebrated samovars or Russian tea-urns; great piles of lumber, granaries full of corn, and huge heaps of bags of salt from the eastern steppes. From one quarter to another, and it seems like visiting vast magazines of merchandise that have been gathered for the subsistence of a great army, and so indeed it is,— the vast army of consumers to whom it is to be distributed,— and this great space, now so crowded with masses of merchandise, would be left in a few weeks a comparatively barren waste and dusty plain.

There is what is known as the Chinese quarter, easily recognized from the peculiar architecture of the shops, but there were no Chinese there, most of the booths being closed, although the other portions of the fair at the time of our visit (last of August) were in full operation.

Pushing our investigations onward, we began to meet Turks, — veritable Turks, turbaned Turks in long robes and colored slippers, — and it really seemed that we were to see the Nijni Novgorod of imagination in reality when we came to a row of cheap wooden shanties, in front of which, with goods displayed, sat two or three Mussulmans in bright-colored robes and white turbans, and we witnessed the introduction of one "true believer" to another in true oriental style, all three looking as if they had just stepped out of a story of the "Thousand and One Nights." The profound salaams given and returned, the good-wishes and various compliments passed, interspersed with other salaams, until the invitation to enter was given, and all three gravely retired to the usual pipes and coffee.

We found we were in a veritable Turkish quarter, for, on turning a corner, there stood, in an enclosed patch of ground, a Turkish mosque. It was surrounded by a dilapidated fence, but intruders were kept at a distance by officials with clubs at the entrances, who allowed none but Mussulmans to enter.

Of course, we were anxious to gain entrance. If you wish to excite an intense desire on the part of the public to inspect premises that you desire to keep free from intrusion, write up "No Admittance" over the door.

It appears that it was some sort of a Mohammedan festival or holyday, and all of the faithful were in their national costume on the occasion.

Our guide, to whom we communicated our desire to see the inside of a mosque, shook his head, and doubted our getting further than the door. The outside guardians were easily corrupted, and we Frenghis or Giaours, or whatever the word was the "true believers" of the Arabian Nights stories used to designate "the infidel," stood within the enclosure, watching an outcoming of Mussulmans from the sacred mosque, at the door of which was stationed another guardian. To him proceeded our guide, and anon he was conversing with the mollah, who came forward, a tall, grave-looking Turk, with beautiful silk-embroidered pelisse, green slippers, high turban, and flowing beard, an ideal Haroun al Raschid, who, as our guide bowed profoundly and pressed his palm, returned a grave salutation, and, with a courteous wave of the hand, caused the guard at the portal to fall back, and invited us to enter and ascend to the place of worship.

A score or more of slippers were at the foot of the little staircase. We were not required to remove our shoes, but, on removing our hats, were politely told it was not required in God's house to uncover the head. The little staircase of ten or twelve steps brought us to a broad landing, from which opened a wide door into an unfurnished circular room, the floor covered with a green carpet. One large window fronted towards the east — the direction of Mecca, the holy city.

The worshippers simply spread their little rugs or mats, knelt facing this great window, with arms crossed upon their breasts, or prostrated themselves, with their foreheads touching the floor, reciting their prayers as they did so.

This was the only service or religious ceremony we saw, and this from outside the door, for no infidel foot could penetrate further. A sturdy official, with stout staff and sour expression of countenance, stood guarding the portal.

We owed the privilege of penetrating thus far, and the few moments at the portal, rarely vouchsafed, to the persuasive eloquence of our guide and the confidential contribution of a few roubles "for the good of the church." Upon our exit we were again reminded of our old friend, the "Thousand and One Nights," by a swarm of Turkish beggars. One man who displayed terrible sores, and another a deformed limb, a third who hobbled upon two stumps close off at the hips, and the frightful dwarf but a few feet high, with big head and harsh voice, all beset us with clamors for alms.

Our guide, who was the only one of the party wearing a tall, glossy hat, was taken for the milord, while our more modest travelling-caps gave us a lower social position in their eyes, for he was at once surrounded by this motley group, who inferred, from his buying admittance into the sacred edifice and the courtesy shown by the mollah, that he must have plenty of money to scatter, and it was with difficulty we forced our way through the noisy crowd to the gate and outside. Here the word had evidently been passed, and a crowd of Russian and Tartar beggars, a howling mob, surrounded us with shrill cries, and we had to run for it and seek shelter in one of the neighboring bazaars, through which we escaped to the point where our carriage was waiting.

The principal portion of the plain on which the fair is held is overflowed in the spring and under water. During the progress of the fair, every precaution is taken against fire, which has previously done much damage, owing to the combustible nature of the cheap buildings. The whole fair-grounds are now surrounded by a canal filled with water, and large sewers pass beneath them, which are kept free and clear by water from the river. No smoking is permitted within the fair limits.

CHAPTER XVII.

The fair has its cheap quarter, where goods of coarse and cheap description are sold to the crowds of workpeople who are here during the season, and one section in particular, which seemed devoted to the sale of cast-off rags and worn-out articles of all nations. It was a sort of rag or rag-and-dust-bin fair of itself, the articles being mainly displayed in little heaps on the ground over the area occupied. Here it seemed as if the dust-bins, dirt-barrels, and rag-bags of the world had been emptied. It is rivalled only by the rag-fair in the streets around and in the vicinity of St. Patrick's Cathedral in Dublin.

Old men were squatted beside a heap of boots and shoes that were mated and mismated, of all sorts and sizes; others presided over what appeared to be a miscellaneous rag-heap, but which proved to be portions and parts of costumes — there was the waist of what was once a gay dress, an old crushed bonnet, a buttonless coat slit up the middle of the back, a red and black stocking tied together as a pair, and an old cape with half the cheap fur trimming torn off, the collection looking as if it had been the aim of its proprietor to obtain as imperfect and damaged an assortment as possible. Another dealer had rusty hinges, nails, door-handles, bolts, and a few worn-out metal tools.

Some had extemporized a counter with two casks and a board, and spread out old cheap dishes and culinary articles; others had built the rudest kind of huts, where they sold rosaries, holy images, candles, etc., of the cheapest description; another had nothing but old bits of curious stone, marble, jasper, and mineralogical specimens, and in his heap of dusty pebbles our guide had the good-fortune to discover a bit of ribbon jasper, a beautiful specimen, which he bought for ten copecks, and affirmed to be worth five roubles in Petersburg.

The place was noisy with the vociferations of both buyers and sellers over their transactions, which varied in amount from two to ten cents, and the miscellaneous character of the crowd rendered the place such a one as we did not care to remain in long.

There was still another feature of the fair which is like the old-time fair, and where the common people, the porters, laborers, workers, and thousand and one hangers-on, amuse themselves evenings, or when not at work. Here were two or three large buildings or hotels, frequented by the cattle drovers, the boatmen, stevedores, etc., and in which prostitutes openly carried on their vocation, engaging their rooms there for the season and sauntering around the rude piazzas or seated there enjoying mugs of tea with their male companions. Scattered all about were cheap dance-houses, raree-shows, penny theatres, dwarfs and giants, drinking-booths and wild-beast exhibitions; and at one point a Russian Punch and Judy show was in progress, surrounded by an admiring crowd.

Desirous of seeing something of this phase of life, we entered one of the most pretentious amusement-places, where the price of admission was five copecks. In the centre of a rough hall was one of those roundabout machines of hobby-horse-headed cars, such as children ride round and round in a circle in at fairs; it was turned by a man at a crank. In this were Russian and Tartar male and female peasants riding round and round, while at the tables, each side of the room, were other dirty specimens of each race, eating bowls of cheap cabbage-soup, drinking beer or the inevitable tea.

A band of what appeared to be Calabrian minstrels, from their costume, mounted a little platform to play their instruments, composed of two rude bagpipes of rough skin, two straight wooden clarinet-looking pipes, and a brass horn. The combination was terrific, and a test of one's endurance amid the clouds of tobacco-smoke, the close atmosphere of the place, mingled with the creaking of the merry-go-round machine and the laughter of its occupants. But when this band ceased and a native Russian band, clad in sheepskins, and with various indescribable instruments, struck up, it seemed

> "As all the fiends from heaven that fell
> Had pealed their banner cry of hell."

and we incontinently fled from the odor of cabbage-soup, tobacco, and nastiness to the outer air.

Another experience in this quarter was more amusing. Terrible pictures of black savages, seated in a circle, devouring white human beings, decorated a sort of side-show-looking booth. These works of art represented one hungry individual gnawing away at a human leg as if it were an ear of corn, and another engaged upon a dissevered arm in the same manner, while a third was striking down a victim, to replenish a huge pot boiling over a big fire. Inscriptions in Russian beneath, according to our guide's translation, told that this was an exhibition of man-eaters, or cannibals, but our curiosity was at once aroused by an inscription in English, and in good Roman characters, beneath one of the pictures, describing them as "Man-eating Savages," and we paid our copecks and entered.

At one end of the tent sat three Australians, or South Sea Islanders, a man, woman, and child, undersized specimens of humanity, and, although the man was got up with ferociously frizzed head, tattooed and painted face, a skewer through his nose, big ear-rings in his ears, and his body naked except a gay-colored cloth around the loins, he did not appear to be a very formidable antagonist.

He began to walk up and down a little railed enclosure, flourishing a boomerang, and squalling some sort of gibberish, which we supposed to be "cannibal language," and we began commenting in our own tongue upon him, when, at the first interchange of sentences, the attention of the other two was immediately attracted, and the countenance of the little warrior, who was near us, underwent a surprising change; his assumed fierceness gave way to a look of surprise, he dropped his boomerang, ran to a curtain at one end of the tent, raised it, and said something to some one within, and, then returning to where we stood, with a lot of cards in his hand, said: —

"Would you like to buy my photograph?"

He gave a shrill laugh at our start of surprise at this civilized speech from a supposed cannibal, and, coming from behind the curtain at that moment, the proprietor of the show addressed us in our own language, asking us if we were not Americans.

We replied in the affirmative.

"So am I," said he. "My name is Cunningham, and this is what they make of it in this country," and he pointed to a name in Russian characters on one of his handbills, that was an undecipherable word nearly a foot long. "I never knew I had such a bad name, till I saw it printed in this detestable place."

"How do you find business here?"

"Business? good for nothing, sir. Just think of running a show like this for five cents admission, and a confounded Punch and Judy outside taking away half your audience. Don't pay, sir! don't pay!"

It seemed that this exhibitor, according to his account, had travelled all over America with Barnum, exhibiting the troupe of "Indian cannibals," originally nine in number, but now reduced by death to these three — the young fellow who spoke English, the little boy, and the woman. He had left Barnum some time since, travelled in Europe on his own account, had a curiosity to see Russia, had seen enough of it, and was now going back to Australia, where he had business, and would "take these poor niggers home," if he "could get them there alive."

"But what killed the others? Change of climate, we suppose?"

"Change of climate! No, they were killed with kindness."

"Kindness!"

"Yes, women who came to the show would feed 'em with sweet cakes and fruit, and they would devour everything given to them, like monkeys. and men thought it sport to smuggle liquor into the tent and give it to them when they got so used to their situation as to walk about a little from the platform and cage we kept them in. Their constitutions are not strong, and the most rigorous care has to be used to preserve their lives, owing to their ignorance in care of themselves, and their eating anything and everything that is offered them."

Our interview ended with a proffer of free admission for the remainder of the season — a space of three or four days — from the exhibitor, and a gift by us of a few copecks to the cannibals, who responded with a "dank you, sar," as we took our leave.

The tea we found everywhere in Russia to be equal to all that has been said of it. Never have I drunk any of such exquisite flavor; and even at the ordinary restaurants it far exceeds any that we usually have in England or America. Various reasons are given for this. One is that caravan tea, brought overland — a long journey of eight or ten months — in its loose, clumsy bundles, is so shaken up as to get rid of its tannin and all dirt and foreign substances, while that that is sent in closely packed boxes by sea does not. Perhaps there may be a good deal in the way the Russians prepare their tea; nevertheless, there are some choice varieties which cost from six to eight dollars a pound there. Nearly a tenth of all the tea sold here, I am told, is grown in northern China, and is brought overland from Kiakhta, a city quite near the border-line of China and Asiatic Russia.

The Russian samovar, of which all travellers speak, is simply a copper urn having a pipe running through it. In this pipe lighted charcoal is placed, which keeps the water hot. At the restaurants this hot water was drawn upon a small quantity of strong solution of tea, in tumblers, that appeared to have been previously prepared, filling the glass to the brim, and then a thin slice of lemon was added. They assert that the yellow tea — as it is called here, on account of its pale color — is seldom exported from Asia or Russia. It is quite delicate in flavor, and steeps strong.

They have curious stories of the tea-poisoning of the

Russian tea-merchants, which are only another version of the effects of continued testing on tea-samples that we have previously read. Indeed, I could but wonder at the power of olfactories and lungs of those I saw in Nijni, who must have inhaled no small quantity of the insidious dust and impalpable powder of the herb as they took deep inhalations of handful after handful from the samples brought to them from hundreds of chests.

The Russian tea-merchants, when present on the Chinese frontier for buying tea, are, it is said, obliged to taste from a hundred and fifty to two hundred specimens of strong tea-infusions daily, do not swallow the infusion, but, nevertheless, a slow intoxication appears in them. The symptoms are loss of appetite, constipation, which alternates with diarrhœa, a failure of general nutrition, periodical epigastric pains, and dryness and sallowness of the skin; hypochondriacal frame of mind, marked failure of memory, and also weakness of visual vacuity, sometimes diplopia, and of taste and smell. With this in prospect, who would desire to be a tea-merchant!

The vodki-shops are not very attractive-looking tippling-places. The furniture of one we looked into consisted of a rude table, in one corner, near which sat the proprietor, and on which were two or three earthen and tin drinking-cups. A couple of demijohns or covered jars of the potent fluid stood near him. Two of his customers were snoring profoundly, in a corner, on an old bit of straw-matting, and three others were seated on a rough board-seat near the door, in various stages of intoxication. Beyond two or three clumsy stools, the colored picture of a saint, stuck up on the wall, and an old soup-tub, there was absolutely no other furniture in the place.

The object of the Russian peasant, when he enters one of these places, seems to be to get drunk as speedily as possible. He therefore drinks cup after cup of liquor, till he falls into a drunken stupor, and is either bundled out of the place or stowed away in a corner, as were the two we saw, to sleep off his potations.

A view of this great fair at its height, and of the enormous quantity of huge freight-steamers, boats, and river-craft that blacken the Volga and Oka, gives one some idea of the vast resources, the enormous wealth, and the commerce of this great empire and its ninety millions of inhabitants. The fair is officially opened the 27th of July, and lasts till about the 1st of September. At the end of that month the seven or eight miles are pretty generally cleared of all merchandise and booths, for later on in the autumn most of the territory is overflowed and under water.

The porters, laborers, boatmen, teamsters are nearly all Tartars, wretchedly clothed, and apparently living anywhere and anyhow. The great merchants of St. Petersburg and other Russian cities have chief clerks or managers here during the season, to look after their interests, and they generally have rooms in the upper part of their warehouses and do their business with each other in a sort of public square, where an exchange is daily held.

At this exchange, and in and about the square in which it is situated, a large crowd of brokers, buyers, dealers, and merchants, of different nationalities, assemble daily, at noon. And, judging from the hum of voices, clatter of different tongues, and the excited gesticulations, all were as eager, sharp, and active in their business transactions as their brethren in European or American capitals. Here we found lumber-merchants, tea-traders, ship-captains, iron-dealers, and grain-shippers, busy settling large transactions, or making their contracts. In grain it appears that the competition of the United States, Australia, and India, which is constantly increasing, has had an injurious effect upon the Russian product. Recent authorities place the average price of the best Russian wheat in St. Petersburg and Odessa as follows: in 1883 at $1.13 per bushel; in 1884 at 95 cents; in 1885 at 90 cents. Rye in the same period fell from 75 cents to 62 cents per bushel, and there was in 1887 but small demand from abroad for Russian wheat, on account of the inferior quality of the crop. Russia is one of the large wheat-producing countries — in fact, the only country in Europe which produces more than it consumes, its annual surplus for export sometimes amounting to sixty million bushels, and yet most of the cereal is sown broadcast, harvested with the sickle, and threshed with the flail. Moreover, three-quarters of the harvest-work is still done by women.

Some idea of the business done at Nijni Novgorod fair, during the two months it is held, may be had from the fact that over eighty million dollars worth of merchandise changes hands, and from one hundred and fifty to one hundred and seventy-five thousand sellers and buyers are in daily attendance.

Many of the Russian merchants were returning home during our visit, and when, at night, we came into the great railroad-station we found quite a crowd awaiting the train to back in for the journey to Moscow. We had half an hour to wait, and, as no seats could be secured in advance, but all must take their chances when the doors were thrown open and the now darkened platforms would be lighted up, our chances for a comfortable night looked ominous.

Our guide, however, was equal to the occasion, and we were quietly piloted away to the farther end of the building, through a dark room, out through a door unlocked by an official, and thence conducted down the track to an unlighted train, and spirited into a choice compartment, which we speedily converted to our own use by putting out the sliding seats, spreading wraps, and extending ourselves for the night.

In fifteen minutes the train was pulled into the station, the lights lighted, and the great doors of the station opened and the crowd of passengers poured in; but a glance at the three foreigners and the limited amount of space was enough for Russians with their sleeping-wraps and pillows, and they made no effort to trench upon the space left in our compartment, and so we rolled on in sole possession till we reached Moscow next day, and considered the five-rouble bribe well expended.

I noticed many of these returning Russian merchants had large bundles of a regular travelling-outfit with them, such as shawls, towels, blankets, pillows, soap, etc., for in the lesser towns the accommodations are so inferior that these become necessities of comfort for him. And on the road between Nijni and Moscow, although a thin stream of water could be drawn upon the hands in the lavatory of the sleeping-cars, neither towel nor soap was provided. The use of water, it is said, is only understood by the average Russian when he takes his weekly parboiling in the Russian bath.

Russian railroad-fares are rather high, and one reason why they are so is that at the close of the Turco-Russian war, in casting about for some means to raise funds to defray the expenses, it was decided to tax railroad-fares — that is, an addition of twenty-five per cent. was made to the price of all railroad-fares in the empire, the addition being appropriated by the government.

I had read in the English story-books so much about the thievish propensity of the Russians that I thought that inquiry of the station-master at Moscow for an umbrella left carelessly on a bench there three nights previously would be a useless effort; nevertheless, it was made, through my guide and interpreter, and, after a description of the missing article, I was invited to step across the street, to the office of one of the officials, where a polite young Russian, with silver braceleted wrist, and who spoke French fluently, restored it, declining anything for the service except my signature of receipt and the name of my hotel.

My experiences at the three cities I have attempted to describe were utterly free from any of that espionage or trouble from police authorities or respecting passports that I had reason to expect in some degree. This may be in part owing to the fact that I was in the hands of the best of guides, a man well known to all the authorities, that we had taken care to have our passports strictly correct, and, last of all, that we were Americans.

One word about passports. These must be always properly *viséd* before departure from Russia, as well as before entering, for no one is allowed to cross the frontier without proper authority so to do; indeed, it may be more difficult to get out of the country than to get into it, if the proper precautions be not taken.

But how it is possible for an individual who understands neither French, German, nor Russian to make his way at all here seems a wonder. The drosky-drivers, of course, know nothing but Russian, and are wonderfully stupid in the interpretation of the language of pantomime. I could hardly blame one, however, whom an American summoned to take him to the railroad-station, and, being unable to tell him his destination, gave an imitation of the locomotive under a head of steam, which so frightened the fellow that he whipped up his horse and hastily drove off to a group of his fellows, pointing back in alarm to the supposed lunatic.

There is no fixed price for the common street-droskies. and a bargain has to be always previously made with the drivers, to prevent imposition.

In some of the great shops in St. Petersburg and Moscow, French and German were spoken, and in many of the smaller ones the latter language by the German Jew proprietors. One is struck, as he goes farther into Russia, by the absence of ladies in the streets; it appears to be an Eastern fashion here, that they have not yet outgrown, for ladies to withdraw from public gaze and be seen as seldom as possible abroad or upon the streets. We saw some fine specimens of tall men, but their colorless, blond faces were in striking contrast to ruddy-cheeked Germans whom one meets immediately after crossing the frontier.

The author's opportunities were necessarily limited in simply making the usual traveller's tour in Russia, from Berlin to Petersburg, to Moscow, to Nijni Novgorod, and their immediate vicinities. They were enough, however, to enable him to obtain some indications of the vast resources of the empire, and to see to what great importance, as regards strength and commercial position, it is slowly but surely rising.

Travelling is now more free and less impeded than formerly. Gas, water, railroads, the telegraph, and other modern improvements, are in use in the great cities, and being introduced into the lesser ones; while a strong middle class, of increasing intelligence and means, is appearing, who will do, and have already done, much to advance and develop their country.

Russia covers an extent of territory half as large as Europe, and over a third of Asia; even Siberia, which of late years is developing mines of enormous value, covers six times the area of England and Scotland.

The Russians are evidently a patriotic people; and the immense military force the empire could bring into the field if the army were put on a war-footing would render Russia one of the most dangerous of foes to encounter.

With an enormous territory as yet undeveloped, with vast tracts of productive grain-growing land, mineral wealth not yet opened that must be almost fabulous in its amount, a tremendous timber-product, vast pasture-lands, good geographical position as regards controlling the commerce of the East, the power which the rulers of Russia are destined to hold in the future must exceed anything even dreamed of by the present generation.

www.ingramcontent.com/pod-product-compliance
Lightning Source LLC
Chambersburg PA
CBHW031745230426
43669CB00007B/492